AF609480

JHARKHAND

A STATE STUDY GUIDE

NEERAJ KUMAR JHA

Published by

Hawk Press
4836/24, Ansari Road, Daryaganj
New Delhi – 110 002
Phones: 91-11-23278618, 91-11-43667199
E-mail: thehawkpress@gmail.com
www.thehawkpress.com

ISBN: 978-93-88318-75-4

Preface

Jharkhand is a state in eastern India, carved out of the southern part of Bihar on 15 November 2000. The state shares its border with the states of Bihar to the north, Uttar Pradesh to the northwest, Chhattisgarh to the west, Odisha to the south and West Bengal to the east. It has an area of 79,710 km (30,778 sq mi).

The movement for a separate state of Jharkhand is a tribulent odessey spread over a century. Triabl uprisings in Bihar during the British rule against exploitation by " DIKUS" (outsiders) grew into a forceful movement for political identity and is headed for its culmination on Tuesday 14th November, 2000 midnight with the creation of a separate Jharkhand state - the 28th in India.

The tribes of Jharkhand consist of 32 tribes (8 primitive) inhabiting the Jharkhand state in India. The tribes in Jharkhand were originally classified on the basis of their cultural types by the Indian, Lalita Prasad Vidyarthi.

Culture of Jharkhand refers to the culture of Indian state of Jharkhand, located in East India and surrounded by states of Bihar, West Bengal, Uttar Pradesh, Chhatisgarh, and Odisha. The culture of Jharkhand is diverse with many languages, ethnic groups, traditions and festivals.

Folk dances of Jharkhand represent its vibrant culture and tradition. There are various folk dance in the state of Jharkhand which are performed during harvest season, festival and social gatherings. Some folk and tribal dances in Jharkhand are Jhumair, Mardana Jhumair, Janani Jhumair, Domkach, Lahasua, Jhumta, Fagua, Painki, Chhau, and Santali.

The constitutional head of the government of Jharkhand

is the governor, who is appointed by the President of India. The real executive power rests with the chief minister and the cabinet. The political party or the coalition of political parties having a majority in the Legislative Assembly forms the government.

Geography of Jharkhand is comprises of the Chota Nagpur Plateau, which is the source of the Koel River, Damodar River, Brahmani River, Kharkai River, and Subarnarekha rivers, whose upper watersheds lie within Jharkhand. Much of the state is still covered by forest. Forest preserves support populations of Royal Bengal Tiger and Asian Elephant.

Jharkhand has the country's two biggest steel plants at Bokaro in the public sector and Tata Iron and Steel Company (TISCO) in Jamshedpur in the private sector. Other important industries are Tata Engineering and Locomotive Company, Sriram Bearing, Usha Martin, Indian Tube Company, etc. The state is abundantly rich in minerals-copper, coal, iron, manganese, mica, chromite, bauxite, etc., and has the potential of becoming one of the most prosperous states of India.

This is a reference book. All the matter is just compiled and edited in nature, taken from the various sources which are in public domain.

The book is of great importance for the scholars, researchers, students, teachers and historians as well pertaining to this sphere.

—Editor

ABOUT THE BOOK

Jharkhand (lit. "Bushland" or The land of forest) is a state in eastern India, carved out of the southern part of Bihar on 15 November 2000. The state shares its border with the states of Bihar to the north, Uttar Pradesh to the northwest, Chhattisgarh to the west, Odisha to the south and West Bengal to the east. It has an area of 79,710 km (30,778 sq mi). The city of Ranchi is its capital and Dumka its sub capital. Jharkhand suffers from resource curse; It accounts for more than 40% of the mineral resources of India, but it suffers widespread poverty as 39.1% of the population is below the poverty line and 19.6% of the children under five years of age are malnourished.The state is primarily rural, with only 24% of the population living in cities. The Government of Jharkhand also known as the State Government of Jharkhand, or locally as State Government, is the supreme governing authority of the Indian state of Jharkhand and its 24 districts. It consists of an executive, led by the Governor of Jharkhand, a judiciary and a legislative branch. Jharkhand politics has been at the center of interest right from early days of the state's creation, following its breakaway form Bihar in 2000. Politics in Jharkhand has an old history. It has been the site of many tribal revolutions right from the British days and it was a similar kind of insurgence that led to the creation of the independent state of Jharkhand. Jharkhand has the country's two biggest steel plants at Bokaro in the public sector and Tata Iron and Steel Company (TISCO) in Jamshedpur in the private sector. Other important industries are Tata Engineering and Locomotive Company, Sriram Bearing, Usha Martin, Indian Tube Company, etc. The book is of great importance for the scholars, researchers, students, teachers and historians as well pertaining to this sphere.

Contents

1

State at a Glance

Jharkhand (lit. "Bushland" or The land of forest) is a state in eastern India, carved out of the southern part of Bihar on 15 November 2000. The state shares its border with the states of Bihar to the north, Uttar Pradesh to the northwest, Chhattisgarh to the west, Odisha to the south and West Bengal to the east. It has an area of 79,710 km (30,778 sq mi).

The city of Ranchi is its capital and Dumka its sub capital.

Jharkhand suffers from resource curse; It accounts for more than 40% of the mineral resources of India, but it suffers widespread poverty as 39.1% of the population is below the poverty line and 19.6% of the children under five years of age are malnourished.The state is primarily rural, with only 24% of the population living in cities.

HISTORY

Stone tools have discovered from Chota Nagpur plateau region which is from Mesolithic and Neolithic period. There are ancient Cave Paintings in Isko, Hazaribagh district which are from Meso-chalcolithic period (9,000-5,000 BC). Several Iron slags, microlith, Potsherds have discovered from Singhbhum district which are from 1400 BCE according to Carbon dating age.

According to writers including Gautam Kumar Bera, there was already a distinct geo-political, cultural entity called Jharkhand even before the Magadha Empire. During the age of Mahajanpadas around 500 BC, Jharkhand state was a part of Magadha, Anga, Banga, Kalinga, Kashi and Vajji. Jharkhand was part of greater Magadha region and was in some way culturally different from Historical Vedic religion.

Samudragupta, while marching through the present-day Chotanagpur region, directed the first attack against the kingdom of Dakshina Kosala in the Mahanadi valley.

Daud Khan, who launched his invasion starting from Patna on 3 April 1660, attacked south of Gaya district and finally arrived at the Palamu Forts on 9 December 1660. The terms of surrender and payment of tribute were not acceptable to the Cheros; Daud Khan wanted complete conversion of all Hindus under the Chero rule to Islam. Following this, Khan mounted a series of attacks on the forts. Cheros defended the forts but ultimately both forts were occupied.

The Chero King Medini Ray (1662–1674), ruled for thirteen years from 1662 to 1674 from Medininagar in Palamau. His rule extended to areas in South Gaya and Hazaribagh. He attacked Navratangarh and defeated the Maharaja of Chhotanagpur.

Following the death of Medini Ray there was rivalry within the royal family of the Chero dynasty which ultimately lead to its downfall; this was engineered by the ministers and advisers in the court. In 1765, the region came under the control of the British East India Company. Chitrajeet Rai's nephew Gopal Rai betrayed him and facilitated the Patna Council of the British East India Company to attack the fort. When the new fort was attacked by Captain Camac on 28 January 1771, the Chero soldiers fought valiantly but had to retreat to the old fort on account of water shortage. This facilitated the British army to occupy the new fort located on a hill without any struggle. This location was strategic and enabled the British to mount canon supply and the old fort was besieged by the British on 19 March 1771. The fort was finally occupied by the British in 1772.

British rule

The Princly states in Chota Nagpur Plateau, came within the sphere of influence of the Maratha Empire, but they became tributary states of British India as a result of the Anglo-Maratha Wars known as Chota Nagpur Tributary States. The subjugation and colonisation of Jharkhand region by the British East India Company resulted in spontaneous resistance from the local people.

The first ever revolt against the landlords and the British government was led by Tilka Manjhi, a Paharia leader in Rajmahal Hills in 1771.Soon after in 1779, the Bhumij tribes rose in arms against the British rule in Manbhum, West Bengal.

Santhal rebellion against Zamindari system during British Company Raj in 1855

In 1807, the Oraons in Barway murdered their big landlord from Srinagar. Munda tribe rose in revolt in 1811 and 1813. The Hos in Singhbhum revolted in 1820, Kol revolt in 1832. The Santhal rebellion broke out in 1855 under the leadership of two brothers Sidhu and Kanhu.

The Cheros and Kharwars again rebelled against the British in 1882 but the attack was repulsed. Then Birsa Munda revolt, broke out in 1895 and lasted till 1900. The revolt though mainly concentrated in the Munda belt of Khunti, Tamar, Sarwada and Bandgaon.

In October 1905, the exercise of British influence over the predominantly Hindi-speaking states of Chang Bhakar, Jashpur, Koriya, Surguja, and Udaipur was transferred from the Bengal government to that of the Central Provinces, while the two Oriya-speaking states of Gangpurand Bonai were attached to the Orissa Tributary States, leaving only Kharsawan and Saraikela answerable to the Bengal governor.

In 1936, all nine states were transferred to the Eastern States Agency, the officials of which came under the direct authority of the Governor-General of India, rather than under that of any Provinces.

Post-independence

The ancient Baidyanath Jyotirlinga Temple in Deoghar

After Indian independence in 1947, the rulers of the states

all chose to accede to the Dominion of India. Changbhakar, Jashpur, Koriya, Surguja and Udaipur later became part of Madhya Pradesh state, but Gangpur and Bonai part of Orissa state, and Kharsawan and Saraikelapart of Bihar state.

After the last Assembly election in the state resulted in a hung assembly, RJD's dependence on the Congress extended support on the precondition that RJD would not pose a hurdle to the passage of the Bihar reorganisation Bill (Jharkhand Bill). Finally, with the support from both RJD and Congress, the ruling coalition at the Centre led by the BJP which had made statehood its mail poll plank in the region in successive polls earlier, cleared the Jharkhand Bill in the monsoon session of the Parliament this year, thus paving the way for the creation of a separate Jharkhand state.

Jharkhand statehood

The dynamics of resources and the politics of development still influence the socio-economic structures in Jharkhand, which was carved out of the relatively under developed southern part of Bihar. According to the 1991 census, the state has a population of over 20 million out of which 28% is tribal while 12% of the people belong to scheduled castes. Jharkhand has 24 districts, 260 blocks and 32,620 villages out of which only 45% have access to electricity while only 8,484 are connected by roads. Jharkhand is the leading producer of mineral wealth in the country after Chhattisgarh state, endowed as it is with vast variety of minerals like iron ore, coal, copper ore, mica, bauxite, graphite, limestone, and uranium. Jharkhand is also known for its vast forest resources.

Naxal insurgency

Jharkhand has been at the centre of the Naxalite-Maoist insurgency. Since the uprising of the Naxalites in 1967, 6,000 people have been killed in fighting between the Naxalites and counter-insurgency operations by the police, and its paramilitary groups such as the Salwa Judum. Despite having a presence in almost 7.80% of India's geographical area (home to 5.50% of India's population), the state of Jharkhand is part of the "Naxal Belt" comprising 92,000 square kilometres, where the highest concentrations of the groups estimated 20,000 combatants fight. Part of this is due to the fact that the state harbours a rich abundance of natural resources, while its people live in abject poverty and destitution. The impoverished state provides ample recruits for the communist insurgents, who argue that they are fighting on behalf of the landless poor that see few benefits from the resource extractions. As the federal government holds a monopoly on sub-surface resources in the state, the tribal population is prevented from staking any claim on the resources extracted from their land. In response, the insurgents have recently begun a campaign of targeting infrastructure related to the extraction of resources vital for Indian energy needs, such as coal.

On 5 March 2007, Sunil Mahato, a member of the national parliament, was shot dead by Naxalite rebels near Kishanpur while watching a football match on the Hindu festival of Holi. His widow, Suman Mahato, the Jharkhand Mukti Morcha candidate, won the Jamshedpur Lok Sabha by-election in September 2007 and served in parliament until 2009.

HISTORY OF RANCHI

Brief History of the District

Earlier the name of the district was Lohardaga. The old district had come into existence after the creation of the non-regulation South - West frontier as a result of the Kol rising in 1831-32. The name of the district was changed in 1899 from Lohardaga to Ranchi after the name of a small village now comprised within the headquarters station.

Early History

In ancient times the tract which corresponds to the district of Ranchi and the neighbouring parganas was in the undisturbed possession of Munda and Oraon tribes and was known to Aryans as Jharkhand or the 'forest territory'. The entire tract was presumably beyond the pale of the direct Hindu influence in ancient India. However, Jarasandh, the mighty emperor of Rajgriha in the Mahabharat period might have exercised some kind of loose supervision over the area. Similarly, Mahapadmanand Agrasen of Magadh, who subdued the entire country upto Orrisa, might have gained some control over Jharkhand as well.

Possibly, the area was included in the Magadh Empire during the reign of Ashoka (273-232 B.C.). With the decline of Mauryan power, King Kharavels of Kalinga led on army through Jharkhand and ransacked Rajgriha and Patliputra. Later, Samudra Gupta (335-380 A.D.) must have passed through the area on his expedition to the Deccan.

The Chotanagpur Raj is believed to have been set up in fifth century A.D. after the fall of the imperial Guptas. Phanimukut was elected the first king It is said that he was found by the Side of a tank under the protection of a Nag (Snake). Hence the dynasty founded by him was named the Nag Dynasty.

Mughal Period

The Chotanagpur plateau was reffered to as Jharkhand by the Muhammedan historians. Throughout the Turko-Afgan period (upto 1526), the area remained virtually free from external influence. It is only with the accession of Akbar to the throne of Delhi in 1556 that Muslims influence penetrated Jharkhand, then known to the Mughals as Kokrah. In 1585, Akbar sent a force under the command of Shahabaz Khan to reduce the Raja of Chotanagpur to the position of a tributary. Kokrah was included in the subah of Bihar, as mentioned in the Ain-I-Akbari.

After the death of Akbar in 1605. The area presumably regained its independence. This necessitated an expedition in 1616 by Ibrahim Khan, Fateh Jang, Governor of Bihar and brother of Queen Noorjahan, Ibrahim Khan defeated and captured Durian Sal, the 46th Raja of Chotanagpur. He was later released by the Emperor and allowed to resume his previous position as an independent Chief. After that the relations between the Moghul Emperors and the Kokra Chiefs continued to be somewhat friendly and peacefully. A stipulated revenue of Rs. 6000/ was regularly paid.

In 1632 Chotanagpur was as Jagir to the Governor at Patna for annual payment of Rs. 1,36,000.00. During the reign of Muhammed Shah (1719-1748). Sar Balland Khan, the Governor of Bihar, marched against the Raja of Chotanagpur and forced his submission. Another expedition was led by Fakhruddoula, Governor of Bihar in 1731. He came to terms with the Raja of Ramgarh who owed allegiance to the Raja of Chotanagpur. The district seems to have enjoyed almost an unbroken peace from 1624 when Durjan Sal was released till the appearance of the British in 1772.

British Period

The Diwani of Bengal, Bihar and Orrisa was granted by Emperor Shah Alam-II to the East India Company in 1765. This Diwani included Chotanagpur as a part of Bihar. The internecing quarrels and depredations of the Raja of Gidhaur, the Raja of Ramgarh and the rival claim between Gopal Rai and Chitrajit Rai for the Kingdom of Palamu led the British take an active interest in the area. In 1771 captain Camac attacked Palamu and put Chitrajit Rai as the Raja. The history of Ranchi for sometime thereafter is interlinked with the history of Palamu, Hazaribagh and Singhbhum.

During the operations of Captain Camac against the Raja of Palamu, Dhupnath Shahi, Raja of Chotanagpur rendered useful service to British. He acknowledged the authority of the company and offered to pay an annual tribute of Rs. 12000 instead of Rs. 6000 fixed under the Muslim rule. However, arrears in payment resulted in an expedition against him in 1773, as a result of which an agreement was reached stipulating enhanced payment of Rs. 15000 per year. The Raja was allowed to retain his hold on the internal administration.

Captain Camac was succeeded in 1780 by Chapman, civilian administrator of Chotanagpur. The so-called conquered provinces, were formed into a district under the name of the Ramgarh Hill Tract in 1780 which lasted till 1863. The district of Ranchi was not directly included in this unit but was added under the designation of Tributory Mahal of Chotanagpur. Chapman was at the same time the Judge and the Magistrate and Collector of the district. There was an Adivasi insurrection at Tamar in 1789 which could be quelled only by the use of force. Sporadic disturbances continued for six years more.

Disputes between the Raja and his brothers led to further disturbance in 1807-1808. A force was sent under Major Roughsedge. The Diwan of the Raja who was primarily responsible for the trouble was apprehended and jailed. The Raja paid up arrears of revenue and settled disputes with his brothers. Six police thanas were also set up in 1809, marking the beginning of end of the feudal authority of the Raja. This also marked the induction of non-tribal revenue collecting agents who later oppressed the aboriginal tenants.

The discontent among the tribal population evidenced in the earlier insurrections, found an outlet in the Kol insurrections of 1831-32. The immediate cause for it was the humiliation caused to Mundas by the Sikh and Muslims Thikadars (intermediaries) in revenue collection.. The Mundas got together in Laukha village near Tamar and plundered and destroyed many villages held in farm by Sikh and Muslim Thikadars. They were overpowered by the forces led by captain Wilkinson in 1832.

Ranchi has attracted many Christian missions which have contributed much to the growth of education in the district. The earliest Christian missionaries reached the district in 1845 and the first conversions of the tribal population to Christianity took place in 1850.

1857 Movement

The 7th and 8th Native companies of the Ramgarh Battalion stationed at Hazaribagh rose in revolt on the 30th July. When news of this reached Col. Dalton (who was then the Commissioner of Ranchi), he sent Lt. Graham with two companies of the Ramgarh Light Infantry, thirty horseman and two guns to disarm the regiment at Hazaribagh. Meanwhile, the insurgents at Hazaribagh Started marching to Ranchi by the road via Badam. Getting news of this, the infantry with Lt.Graham also rose against British authority and lcommenced their return journey to Ranchi. Lt. Graham proceeded to Hazaribagh with the cavalry which remained loyal to him and reached there on the 2nd August. The deserters from Lt. Graham's contigent returned to the army station at Doranda and successfully exhorted the Sepoys there to rise against British authority. In view of this, Col. Dalton left Ranchi for Hazaribagh. The insurgent troops at Doranda burnt the offices and Courts of the district office and some bungalows and set free the prisoners in jail.

They expected the insurgents from Hazaribagh to join them but when the latter did not reach Doranda, they set out in the third week of September to join Babu Kuer Singh in Shahabad. They were attacked and defeated on the 2nd October, 1857 at Chatra under a British force commanded by Major English. Meanwhile, Col. Dalton returned to Ranchi on 22nd September with a contingent of force. The courts were reopened and peace and order restored.

Main Events after 1857

The infiltration of the British in the political horizon of Chotanagpur also synchronized with a great socio-economic revolution. Agrarian discontent against the imposition of begari (forced labour) and illegal enhancement of rent by the intermediaries resulted in the Sardari agitation, so called due to the instigation and leadership provided by the Sardars. By

1887 the movement had grown and many Mundas and Oraon cultivators refused to pay rent to the landlords.

The Sardari agitation (or Larai as it was called) was at its height in 1895 when a socio-religious leader named Birsa Munda appeared on the scene. The importance of his role in the social history of Ranchi is borne out by the appllation of Birsa Bhagwan given to him.

The movement led by Birsa Munda was half agrarian and half religious, it had a direct connection with agrarian unrest and also appeared to have been influenced by Christian ideas. Birsa Munda was an apostate from Christianity. His teaching was partly spiritual, partly revolutionary. He proclaimed that the land belonged to the people who had reclaimed it from forests, and therefore, no rent should be paid for it. He asserted that he was the Messiah and claimed divine powers of healing.

Birsa's crusade brought about an armed rising of the deluded peasantry which was quickly suppressed. Birsa died in the jail in 1900. A regious movement among the Oraons was initiated by Jatra Oraon of Bishunpur police station in 1914. The Tana Bhagat movement, as it was called, also had its genesis in agrarian issues and particularly the economic disparity between Christian converts and the traditional or sansari Oraons. The non-Cooperation movement launched by Jatra Oraon and his associates soon spread even to Palamu and Hazaribagh.

The district played an important role in the national freedom movement. Under the guidance of Ganesh Chandra Ghosh Ranchi became an important centre of work for the follower's of Revolutionary party. Ranchi was the venue of a meeting between Mahatma Gandhi and Sir Edward Albert Gait, Lieutenant Governor of Bihar and Orrisa on 4th June and again on 22nd Sept. 1917 in the context of the Champaran Indigo planters repressive measures against the raiyats of that district. The Champaran agrarian law subsequently passed under the name of Bihar and Orrisa Act-I of 1918. The non-Cooperation movement in Ranchi district followed the pattern as elsewhere in India. The movement caught the imagination of the people particularly the Tana Bhagats and a large number of them attended the Gaya session of the congress in December 1922 which was presided over by Deshbandhu Chittranjan Das. These Tana Bhagats returned home deeply impressed with the message of freedom Movement. Barefooted they used to trek over long distances with congress flags in their hands and they carried the message to the masses in the interior. They attended the meetings organized by the non-cooperation workers.

On 5th October, 1926, a khadi exhibition was opened at Ranchi in presence of Sri Rajendra Prasad in the local Arya Samaj Hall. The Tana Bhagats also attended it. This was a part of the constructive programme launched by Mahatma Gandhi after he had suspended the non-cooperation Movement in 1922. The Simon Commission was boy-cotted in 1927. On 4th Aprill, 1930, Tarun Singh (Youth league) of Ranchi organized a meeting in the local municipal park which was attended by a large number of students from different educational institutions. The leaders appealed to them to join the Civil Disobedience Movement.

The Salt Satyagrah which was launched at the behest of Mahatma Gandhi, received great response in Ranchi District. In the wake of the quit India Revolution of 1942 the arrest of national leaders led to strikes, processions, demonstrations and also disruption of the lines of communications. The district took an active part in the Subsequent events which led to country's indepedence in 1947.

FREEDOM STRUGGLE

Baba Tilka Majhi

Santal Hero: Baba Tilka Majhi was first Santal leader who took up the arms against the British in the 1789's. The British surrounded the Tilapore forest from which he operated but he and his men held the enemy at bay for several weeks. When he was finally caught in 1784, he was tied to the tail of a horse and dragged all the way to the collector's residence at Bhgalpur. There, his lacerated body was hung from a Banyan tree. A statue to the heroic leader was erected at the spot after independence.

Hul

Hul is a Santali term. It means a movement for liberation. Santals in Santal Paraganas (presently in the State of Jharkhand) belongs to Santali tribe. Two Murmu brothers, Sido and Kanhu.

Santal Hul was one of the fiercest battles in the history of Indian freedom struggles causing greatest number of loss of lives in any battles during that time. The number of causalities of Santal Hul was 20,000 according to Hunter who wrote it in annals of Rural Bengal. The Santal Hul of 1855-57 was master minded by four brothers Sidhu, Kahnu, Chand and Bhairav; a heroic episode in India's prolonged struggle for freedom. It was, in all probability, the fiercest liberation movement in India next to Great Sepoy Mutiny in 1857.

With the capture of political power of India by the East India Company, the natural habitats of the Adivasi (indigenous) people including the Santals began to shatter by the intruders like moneylenders. Traders and revenue farmers, who descended upon them in large numbers under the patronage of the Company.

Believe it or not, the rate of interest on loan to the poor and illiterate Santals varied from 50% to 500%. These intruders were, needless to mention the crucial links in the chain of ruthless exploitation under colonial rule. They were the instruments through which the indigenous groups and tribes were brought within the influence and control of the colonial economy.

Discontent had been simmering in the Santal Paraganas (presently in Jharkhand) from the early decades of the nineteenth century owing to most naked exploitation of the indigenous Santals by both the British authorities and their collaborators, native immigrants.

Sido Murmu and Kanhu Murmu, hailing from the village Bhognadih in Sahibganj district, had long been brooding over the injustices perpetrated by the oppressors like hundreds and hundreds of their tribe's men. The situation finally reached a flash point and, not surprisingly, a small episode that took place in July 1855 triggered one of the fiercest uprisings that the British administration ever faced in India.

The emergence of Sido and Kanhu, youthful, dynamic and charismatic, provided a rallying point for the Santals to revolt against the oppressors. On 30th June 1855, a large number of Santals assembled in a field in Bhagnadihi village of Santal Paragana, They declared themselves as free and took oath under the leadership of Sido Murmu and Kanhu Murmu to fight unto the last against the British rulers as well as their agents.

Militant mood of the Santals frightened the authority. A Police agent confronted them on the 7th July and tried to place the Murmu brothers under arrest.

The angry crowd reacted violently and killed the Police agent and his companions. The event sparked off a series of confrontations with the Company's Army and subsequently reached the scale of a full-fledged war.

At the outset, Santal rebels, led by Sido and Kanhu, made tremendous gains and captured control over a large tract of the country extending from Rajmahal hills in Bhagalpur district to Sainthia in Birbhum district. For the time being, British rule in this vast area became completely paralyzed.

Many moneylenders and native agents of the Company were killed. Local British administrators took shelter in the Pakur Fort to save their life. However, they rebel could not hold on to their gains due to the superior fire power of the East India Company came down heavily on them.

The courage, chivalry and sacrifice of the Santals were countered by the rulers with veritable butchery. Out of 50,000 Santal rebels, 15,000 20,000 were killed by the British Indian Army. The Company was finally able to suppress the rebellion in 1856, though some outbreaks continued till 1857.

The Santals showed great bravery and incredible courage in the struggle against the military. As long as their national drums continued beating, the whole party would stand and allow themselves to be shot down. There was no sign of yielding. Once forty Santals refused to surrender and took shelter inside a mud house. The troops surrounded the mud house and fired at them but Santals replied with their arrows. Then Soldiers made big hole through muddy wall, and the Captain ordered them surrender but they again shot a volley of arrows through the hole and Captain again asked them to surrender but they continued shooting arrows.

Some of the soldiers were wounded. At last when the discharge of arrows from the door slackened, the Captain went inside the room with soldiers. He found only one old man grievously wounded, standing erect among the dead bodies. The soldier asked him to throw away arms, but instead he rushed on him and killed him with his battle axe.

It is believed that Sido was captured by the British forces through treachery and Kanhu through an encounter at Uparbanda. And was subsequently killed in captivity. The Santal Hul, however, did not come to an end in vain. It had a long-lasting impact. Santal Parganas Tenancy Act was the outcome of this struggle, which dished out some sort of protection to the indigenous people from the ruthless colonial exploitation. The understanding the mistake, tired to appease the Santals by removing the genuine grievances. Santal territory was born. The regular police was abolished and the duty of keeping peace and order and arresting criminals was vested in the hands of parganait and village headman. Forgotten struggles and so is the unsung Heros ! The brave freedom struggles by Adivasi, specially

Santals (Details, Santals Huls), against the British tyranny and cruelty of Desi (native) landlords have often gone unnoticed and sometimes, by nefarious design excluded from History text books. However, mere omission from the History books in educational curriculum, can not conceal the stories of bravery of Adivasi Heros and stiff resistance, they had offered in the struggles.

But creation of Jharkhand state, which came into existence on 14.11.2000, gives us opportunities to recall our history and unfolds plenty of untold stories, more often than not, excluded in text books. Consequently, to understand the bravery of Adivasi, there is need to deep understanding the History of formation of Jharkhand state, which inextricably mixed with Adivasi freedom struggles dates back to British period. Here is a list of brief events, which marked the way to new state, Jharkhand.

HISTORICAL BACKGROUND OF JHARKHAND

Since Stone age human inhabited in present Jharkhand state. There have several copper tools discovered which are from Chalcolithic period. This area enter in Iron Age during mid 2nd Millenium BCE. According to writers including Gautam Kumar Bera, there was already a distinct geo-political, cultural entity called Jharkhand even before the MagadhaEmpire. Bera's book (page 33) also refers to the Hindu epic Bhavishya Purana.

Prehistoric era

Stone tools and Microlith have discovered from Chota Nagpur plateau region which are from Mesolithic and Neolithic period. There are ancient Cave Paintings in Isko, Hazaribagh district which are from Meso-chalcolithic period (9,000–5,000 BC). There is a group of megaliths found close to Barkagaon that is about 25 km from Hazaribagh at Punkri Barwadih, which has been proven to date back to beyond 3000 BCE.

Copper Hoard Culture

Copper Hoards describe find-complexes which occur in the

northern part of India. These occur mostly in hoards large and small and are believed to date to the later 2nd millennium BCE, although very few derive from controlled and dateable excavation contexts. Characteristic hoard finds from Chota Nagpur Plateau include finely worked pieces, and mostly look at first like axe-heads but are probably ingots.

Iron age(c. 1800 – c. 200 BCE)

Barudih in the Singhbhum district of Jharkhand, yielded evidence of microlith, Neolithic Celts, Iron slags, Wheel made pottery, iron objects include a sickle. The earliest radio carbon dating give a range of 1401 – 837 BCE for this site.

During the age of Mahajanpadas around 500 BC, India saw the emergence of 16 large states that controlled the entire Indian subcontinent. In those days the Jharkhand state was a part of Magadha, Anga, Banga, Kalinga, Kashi and Vajji. In mouryan period, this region was ruled by a number of states, which were collectively known as the Atavika (forest) states. These states accepted the suzerainty of the Maurya Empire during Ashoka's reign (c.232 BCE). According to Indologist Johannes Bronkhorst, the culture of Magadhawas in some ways different than the Vedic kingdoms of the Indo-Aryans.

Early modern period (c. 1526 – 1858 CE)

In Akbarnama the region of Chhotanagpur is described as Jharkhand (Jangal Pradesh). The Jharkhand region was famous by another name Khukhra during the Mughal period which was famous for its Diamonds. Akbar was informed of a rebel Afghan sardar, Junaid Kararani, was taking shelter in Chotanagpur. Besides, the emperor also got information of diamonds being found in this area. Consequently, Akbar ordered Shahbaz Khan Turbani to attack Kokhra (the then seat of Nagvanshi kings and capital of Chotanagpur). At that time Raja Madhu Singh, the 42nd Nagvanshi king was ruling at Kokhra. Consequently Kokhra was subdued by the armies of Akbar and a sum of rupees six thousand was fixed as its annual revenues payable to the Mughals. Till the reign of Akbar, Chotanagpur had not come under the suzerainty of the Mughals and the Nagvanshi rulers had been ruling over this region as independent rulers.

By the advent of the reign of Jahangir, Nagvanshi Raja Durjan Sal had come to power in Chotanagpur. He refused to pay the rent fixed by the Emperor Akbar. Jahangir ordered Ibrahim Khan (governor of Bihar) to attack Kokhra.

The details of this invasion are mentioned in Jahangir's memoirs, Tuzk-e-Jahangiri. There was also another reason behind the invasion. This was the acquisition of the diamonds found in the bed of the Sankh River in the region. Due to its diamonds Chotanagpur was also known as Heera Nagpur and its Raja Durjan Sal, being an expert of diamonds, was known as Heera Raja among the people. Thus to subdue the Raja of Chotanagpur and to acquire valuable diamonds, Jahangir decided to invade chotanagpur. On getting orders from the emperor, Ibrahim Khan marched against Kokhra in 1615 AD.

He entered the Nagvanshi territories easily with the help of his guides. The Nagvanshi Raja Durjan Sal found himself beleaguered himself within the hills and vales. He fled and was at last found in a cave with some of his family members. He was arrested and all diamonds which were in the possession of Durjan Sal and his family were captured by Ibrahim Khan. Twenty four elephants also fell into the hands of Ibrahim Khan. After this, Kokhara was subdued and the diamonds found there were sent to the Imperial court. After his defeat and arrest, Durjan Sal offered as ransom jewels, gold and silver to the value of crores of rupees, but Ibrahim Khan did not release him and took him as a captive to Patna. From there he was sent to the Imperial court and subsequently imprisoned in the fort of Gwalior.

According to Nagvanshi traditions and Col. Dalton, Raja Durjan Sal's confinement lasted twelve years. Ultimately, the very diamonds which had caused the misfortune of Durjan Sal secured him his release and former prosperity. It so happened that from some place, two very large diamonds were brought to Emperor Jahangir's court. A doubt arose in the mind of the Emperor over the genuineness of one of them.

As no one in his court was able to confirm or relieve his suspicion, the Heera Raja was brought to the Imperial court from his incarceration. When the two diamonds were brought before him, he without any hesitation pointed out the fake one. To prove it to the court and the Emperor, he requested two rams to be brought to the court. He then tied the two diamonds on the horns of the two rams and made them fight each other. As a result of the fight, the fake diamond shattered but there was no scratch on the pure one.

The Emperor was so impressed and pleased with Durjan Sal that he not only released him but also restored the prosperity taken from him in addition to his kingdom. The generous Durjan Sal further begged the Emperor to release the other Rajas who had been his companions in prison and his prayer was granted. Being pleased with Durjan Sal, Jahangir conferred the title of 'Shah' on the Kokhra ruler.

On his return to Chotanagpur, Durjan Sal assumed the title of Maharaja and changed his surname. Most probably from that time 'Shah' was added with the names of the Nagvanshi kings. The reign of Durjan Sal lasted for about thirteen years. He died in 1639 or 1640 AD.

Daud Khan, who launched his invasion starting from Patna on 3 April 1660, attacked south of Gaya district and finally arrived at the Palamu Forts on 9 December 1660. The terms of surrender and payment of tribute were not acceptable to the Cheros; Daud Khan wanted complete conversion of all Hindus under the Chero rule to Islam. Following this, Khan mounted a series of attacks on the forts. Cheros defended the forts but ultimately both forts were occupied by Daud Khan, and the Cheros fled to the jungles. Hindus were driven out, the temples were destroyed, and Islamic rule imposed.

In Palamu district, the old fort in the plains, was built by the King of Raksel Rajput Dynasty. However, it was during the reign of King Medini Ray (1662–1674), who ruled for thirteen years from 1662 to 1674 from Medininagar in Palamau, the old fort was rebuilt into a defensive structure. Ray was a Chero king. His rule extended to areas in South Gaya and Hazaribagh. He attacked Navratangarh (33 miles (53 km) from Ranchi) and defeated the Maharaja of Chhotanagpur. With war bounty he constructed the lower fort close to Satbarwa, and this fort became famous in the history of the district.

Following the death of Medini Ray there was rivalry within the royal family of the Chero dynasty which ultimately lead to its downfall; this was engineered by the ministers and advisers in the court. In 1765, the region came under the control of the British East India Company. Chitrajeet Rai's nephew Gopal Rai betrayed him and facilitated the Patna Council of the British East India Company to attack the fort. When the new fort was attacked by Captain Camac on 28 January 1771, the Chero soldiers fought valiantly but had to retreat to the old fort on account of water shortage. This facilitated the British army to occupy the new fort located on a hill without any struggle. This location was strategic and enabled the British to mount canon supported attacks on the old fort. The Cheros fought valiantly with their own canons but the old fort was besieged by the British on 19 March 1771. The fort was finally occupied by the British in 1772.

MOVEMENT FOR SEPARATE STATE

The movement for a separate state of Jharkhand is a tribulent odessey spread over a century. Triabl uprisings in Bihar during the British rule against exploitation by " DIKUS" (outsiders) grew into a forceful movement for political identity and is headed for its culmination on Tuesday 14th November, 2000 midnight with the creation of a separate Jharkhand state - the 28th in India.

The Birsha Munda movement of 1985 - 1900 was the most important among early uprisings against exploitation of the original inhibitants by non-tribal landowners and money landers. Munda succeeded in getting the British to prevent, or at least, minimise alienation of tribal land. A landmark in the movement was the formation of the Chhotanagpur Unnati Samaj in 1915, which acquired political overtones with the demand for a sub-state for the adivasis. The demand was, however, turned down by the Simon commission.

The next important step was the formation of the Adivasis Mahasabha, which saw non-tribals coming out openly in support of the movement for the creation of a separate state. Among those who spearheaded the Jharkhand movement was Jaipal Singh, an Oxford - returned tirbal Christian who helped the regional aspiration gain national recognition.

The Adivasis Mahasabha was rechristened the Jharkhand party here in 1949 under the leadership of Jaipal Singh.

It was with the emergence of this party that the Jharkhand movement bacame purely political. The Jharkhand party became the largest opposition party in the Bihar Assembly winnig all the 32 seats from south Bihar and giving fresh impetus to the government for a separate state.

Considering its growing strength, the Congress started efforts for engineering a split in the Jharkhand Party. As a cosequence, Jaipal Singh fell into its trap and joined the Congress with his followers in 1963. N. E. Horo, a close associates of Jaipal Singh, however, refused to join the Congress and kept the Jharkhand flag flying. But the loss of the Jharkhand Party veterans, who joined the Congress, proved too much for the pro-statehood forces whose strength steadily eroded in successive elections since 1969.

The movement again recieved a shot in the arm with the emergence of the Jharkhand Mukti Morcha in 1972.

The growing strength of the JMM was reflected in the Lok

Sabha and Assembly elections and the demand for a statehood for the first time shook the corridors of power with the then prime minister of India Mr. Rajiv Gandhi setting up a Committee on Jharkhand Matters (CoJM).

In the light of the recommendations by the CoJM, prolonged negotiations between the Centre, the Bihar government and the movement leaders led to the setting up of the Jharkhand Area Autonomous Council (JAAC) in August 1995. It was hailed as a major step towards the creation of Jharkhand.

Buckling under pressuer from the JMM memebers, with whose support the RJD had a majority in the state Assembly, the Bihar government on July 22, 1997 adopted a resolution for the creation of a sepaarate state. In 1998, however, RJD supremeo Mr. Laloo Prasad Yadav reversed his stand on Jharkhand statehood. The JMM reacted sharply, withdrawing its support to the RJD government.

After the last Assembly election in the state threw up a hung Assembly, RJD's dependence on the Congress extended support on the precondition that RJD will not pose a hurdle to the passage of the Bihar recorganisation Bill (Jharkhand Bill).

Ultimately, with the support from both RJD and Congress, the ruling coalition at the Centre led by the BJP which has made statehood its mail poll plank in the region in seccessive polls earlier, cleared the Jharkhand Bill in the monsoon session of the the Parliament this year, thus paving the way for the creation of a separate Jharkhand state.

Jharkhand historiography owes its works to individuals coming from three distinct interests. The British Administrators turned anthropologist turned historians, the Christian Missionaries, the Indian anthropologist cum historians (mainstream cum non Adivasi). Their works have made a significant contribution to the recordings of Jharkhand history, considering the fact that the subjects of their records used oral and other non written means to transfer knowledge from generation to generation.

Written during a period of 'anthropologic' excitement certain important facets of this period seem missing from these written records. The full glory of the Adivasi period, pre Brahamanic, Mogul, British, is missing. Present writings suggest that Jharkhand history too is a victim of the Eurocentric - Judeo Christian biases, as well as the racial/caste biases of Indian historians. When this is one day written we may be enlightened and challenged on our present concepts of civilization and modern science.

What has been the contribution of Adivasi knowledge systems to Indian mainstream culture, language and beliefs? No parallels have been drawn from the fact that Buddhism, Jainism took birth in this very homeland. If such great spiritual movements existed here then in what way were they influenced by the Adivasi genius? In what way did the Adivasi knowledge system of plants and herbs contributed to Ayurvedha or other traditional medical systems of India? The fact that Adivasi metallurgy existed in pre Aryan period has not been even acknowledged. These questions need answering.

Iron smelting was already in practice in 1000 BC around the Subarnarekha River in present day (East) Singhbhum District of Jharkhand according to historian D. C. Chakroboti. Prof DD Koshambi too refers to the fact that besides pastoral lands one of the other reasons for the east wards drive of the Aryan influx culminating with the Mahabharata (700 BC) was the control of metals. If the above is correct then it means that Jharkhand region even before it received its present political identity was already a battle ground between the Adivasis (first people) and outside forces or colonizers. It also means that besides pastoral lands and forest the colonizers came here for the immense knowledge systems in existing including Adivasi metallurgy.

The fact that Gautam Buddha received enlightenment after

receiving hospitality and observing the life of the Mundas Adivasis has not received any recognition by historians. Even though this fact is mentioned in the Pali Canon of Gautama Buddha "Thus I continued in the search for the State of Peace which is beyond understanding - the state of nirvana. Eventually I came to the village of Senani at Uruvela.

There I found a delightful forest, with a river of clear water flowing through it. There was a ford across the river. So I decided to sit in seclusion of the far side of the river, and come back to the village each day for food. While I was there, I attained enlightenment; and I knew that at the end of this life I shall enter nirvana. Thus I broke free from all suffering - from old age, illness, death, grief and corruption. I broke free from the cycle of birth, death and rebirth. I realized that my final birth had already occurred and that I had no future bodily life to endure." Ariyapariyesanna Sutta: Majjhima Nikaya 1.166-167, 175.

Senani at Uruvela are on the banks of the Lilarjan and Phalgu river which meets at Phalgu that exist today they were a part of the Munda country one of the largest tribal group to settle in Jharkhand. Thus it becomes clearer today that Jharkhand historiography is a victim of the racial and caste biases of the dominant forces that ruled and rule this region..

Jharkhand or the 'green forest tract' (rainforest) is an ancient name. Geographically in comprises the plateau region known as Chotanagpur Plateau. It cuts across the North Eastern portion of the central Indian peninsular. The first political reference to Jharkhand goes back to the 13th century when a King of North Orissa by the name Jay Singh Deo, declared himself the King of Jharkhand. The great Vaishnav reformer Chaitanya of the 15th century on his way from Nilaanchal (Orissa) to Mathura (U.P.) also refers to this land as Jharkhand. What ever the nomenclature the first settlers here were the Adivasi Peoples from over 40 different clans or groups (tribes). Jharkhand was and is their homeland.

During the Mogul rule in India there was no definite territorial identity of Jharkhand. But throughout the Mogul rule the name Jharkhand appears to have survived even though the Moguls preferred to this region as 'Kokrah'. It was the British East India Company that set the ball of territoriality of Jharkhand rolling with the receipt of the grant of dewani from the Mogul rulers in 1765.

The entry of the British was met with a strong and stubborn resistance movements by the Adivasi Peoples, forcing them to declare a separate administrative system called the South West Frontier Agency. Jharkhand thus remained a 'partially excluded' area with a different administrative system (from the rest of the British territories) thus respecting and maintaining its separate identity.

The British were not the first to colonize Jharkhand. There are ruins of a number of Buddhist and Jain temples spread all over Jharkhand. More research needs to be done on this. The British and their imposition of the Bengal Permanent Regulation in 1793 was to Institutalise domination that was the beginning of the end of the glory of the Adivasi period. Their decentralized self village governance through their traditional administrative systems according to the different Adivasi communities was threatened. British rule divided the region into Districts and land became subject to systematic taxation for the first time in history. This led to internal division and factionalism resulting in a series of uprising, ethnic in the beginning but eventually becoming pan-Adivasi and regional in character.

The need for the British to crush this hundred year resistance was primarily aimed at the forest and mineral wealth of the region besides its geostatic position amidst the different regions of India. Thus the ground was prepared for extractive industries to enter and plunder. This was further propounded with the 'planned economy' of Independent India and their constructions of the 'temples' of Modern India *i.e.* the Steel Cities, Mega Mining Towns, Timber Mills, Railway network etc.

It should not be seen as a penetration of capital but the penetration of the modes of Capitalism and Capital was in fact created and extracted. If any benefits came with this out flow of capital it was in enclaves, carefully keeping the majority of the Adivasi Peoples apart, and this goes on to this day. The Jharkhand Movement today continues to have its roots in these uprisings.

Jharkhand region today encompasses the Adivasi habitations and mineral and forest regions of Orissa, West Bengal and Chhattisgarh States. However in November 2000, when the Central Government passed legislation for the creation of the Jharkhand State they were careful enough to include only those parts of Jharkhand that came within the State of Bihar.

The word Jharkhand, meaning "forest region," applies to a forested mountainous plateau region in eastern India, south of the Indo-Gangetic Plain and west of the Ganga's delta in Bangladesh. The term dates at least to the sixteenth century. In the more extensive claims of the movement, Jharkhand comprises seven districts in Bihar, three in West Bengal, four in Orissa, and two in Madhya Pradesh. Ninety percent of the Scheduled Tribes in Jharkhand live in the Bihar districts. The tribal peoples, who are from two groups, the Chotanagpurs and the Santals, have been the main agitators for the movement.

Jharkhand is mountainous and heavily forested and, therefore, easy to defend. As a result, it was traditionally autonomous from the central government until the seventeenth century when its riches attracted the Mughal rulers. Mughal administration eventually led to more outside interference and a change from the traditional collective system of land ownership to one of private landholders.

These trends intensified under British colonial rule, leading to more land being transferred to the local tribes' creditors and the development of a system of "bonded labour," which meant permanent and often hereditary debt slavery to one employer.

Unable to make effective use of the British court system, tribal peoples resorted to rebellion starting in the late eighteenth century.

In response, the British government passed a number of laws in the nineteenth and twentieth centuries to restrict alienation of tribal lands and to protect the interests of tribal cultivators.

The advent of Christian missions in the region in 1845 led to major cultural changes, which were later to be important in the Jharkhand movement. A significant proportion of the tribes converted to Christianity, and schools were founded for both sexes, including higher institutions to train tribal people as teachers.

Jharkhand's mineral wealth also has been a problem for the tribes. The region is India's primary source of coal and iron. Bauxite, copper, limestone, asbestos, and graphite also are found there. Coal mining began in 1856, and the Tata Iron and Steel Factory was established in Jamshedpur in 1907.

The modern Jharkhand movement dates to the early part of the twentieth century; activity was initially among Christian tribal students but later also among non-Christians and even some nontribals. Rivalries developed among the various Protestant churches and with the Roman Catholic Church, but most of the groups coalesced in the electoral arena and achieved some successes on the local level in the 1930s. The movement at this period was directed more at Indian dikus (outsiders) than at the British. Jharkhand spokesmen made representations to British constitutional commissions requesting a separate state and redress of grievances, but without much success.

Independence in 1947 brought emphasis on planned industrialization centering on heavy industries, including a large expansion of mining. A measure of the economic importance of the Jharkhand mines is that the region produces more than 75 percent of the revenue of Bihar, a large state.

The socialist pattern of development pursued by the central government led to forced sales of tribal lands to the government, with the usual problem of perceived inadequate compensation. On the other hand, government authorities felt that because the soils of the region are poor, industrialization was particularly necessary for the local people, not just for the national good. However, industrial development brought about further influx of outsiders, and local people considered that they were not being hired in sufficient numbers.

The nationalization of the mines in 1971 allegedly was followed by the firing of almost 50,000 miners from Jharkhand and their replacement by outsiders. Land was also acquired by the government for building dams and their reservoirs.

However, some observers thought that very little of the electricity and water produced by the dams was going to the region. In addition, government forestry favored the replacement of species of trees that had multiple uses to the forest dwellers with others useful only for commercial sales. Traditional shifting cultivation and forest grazing were restricted, and the local people felt that the prices paid by the government for forest products they gathered for sale were too low. In the decades since independence, these problems have persisted and intensified.

On the political front, in 1949 the Jharkhand Party, under the leadership of Jaipal Singh, swept the tribal districts in the first general elections. When the States Reorganisation Commission was formed, a memorandum was submitted to it asking for an extensive region to be established as Jharkhand, which would have exceeded West Bengal in area and Orissa in population.

The commission rejected the idea of a Jharkhand state, however, on the grounds that it lacked a common language. In the 1950s, the Jharkhand Party continued as the largest opposition party in the Bihar legislative assembly, but it gradually declined in strength. The worst blow came in 1963 when Jaipal Singh merged the party into the Congress without consulting the membership. In the wake of this move, several splinter Jharkhand parties were formed, with varying degrees of electoral success. These parties were largely divided along tribal lines, which the movement previously had not seen.

There also has been dissention between Christian and non-Christian tribal people because of differences in level of education and economic development. Non-Christian tribals formed separate organizations to promote their interests in the 1940s and again in the 1960s.

In 1968 a parliamentary study team visited Ranchi investigating the removal of groups from the official list of Scheduled Tribes (thereby depriving these groups of various compensatory privileges). Mass meetings were held and petitions submitted to the study team maintaining that Christians had ceased to be tribals by conversion from tribal religions, and that they benefitted unfairly both from mission schooling and from government protection as members of Scheduled Tribes. In the following years, there were accusations that the missionaries were foreign outside agitators.

In August 1995, the state government of Bihar established the 180-member Provisional Jharkhand Area Autonomous Council. The council has 162 elected members (two each from eighty-one assembly constituencies in the Jharkhand area) and eighteen appointed members.

TRIBES OF JHARKHAND

The tribes of Jharkhand consist of 32 tribes (8 primitive) inhabiting the Jharkhand state in India. The tribes in Jharkhand were originally classified on the basis of their cultural types by the Indian, Lalita Prasad Vidyarthi. His classification was as follows:

- Hunter-gatherer type — Birhor, Korwa, Hill Kharia
- Shifting Agriculture — Sauria Paharia

- Simple artisans — Mahli, Lohra, Karmali, Chik Baraik
- Settled agriculturists — Santhal, Munda, Oraon, Ho, Kharia, Bhumij etc.

Demography

The Scheduled Tribe (ST) population of Jharkhand State is as per 2011 census 8,645,042(Others including Sarna-4,012,622,Christian-1,338,175) of the total population (32,988,134) of the State. Among all States and UTs, Jharkhand holds 6th and 10th ranks terms of the ST population and the percentage share of the ST population to the total population of the State respectively. The growth of the ST population has been 17.3 per cent which is lower by 6 percentage point if compared with the growth of the State's total population (23.3 per cent)during 1991-2001. The state has a total of thirty (30) Scheduled Tribes and all of them have been enumerated at 2001 census. The Scheduled Tribes are primarily rural as 91.7per cent of them reside in villages. District wise distribution of ST population shows that Gumla district has the highest proportion of STs (68.4per cent). The STs constitute more than half of the total population in Lohardaga and Pashchimi Singhbhum districts whereas Ranchi and Pakaur districts have 41.8 – 44.6 per cent tribal population. Kodarma district (0.8 percent) preceded by Chatra (3.8 per cent) has the lowest proportion of the STs Population. Jharkhand has 32 tribal groups:

Literacy and educational level

The overall literacy rate among the STs has increased from 27.5 per cent at 1991 census to 40.7 per cent at 2001census. Despite this improvement, the literacy rate among the tribes is much below in comparison to that of all STs at the national level (47.1per cent). Like the overall literacy rate among the STs, male and female literacy rates (54 per cent and 27.2 per cent) are also considerably lower than those at the national level (59.2 per cent & 34.8 per cent). Among the numerically larger tribes, Oraon and Kharia have more than half of the population in the age of seven (7) years and above are literates while Munda have the literacy rate almost equal to that of all STs at the national level.

Remaining five larger tribal groups have shown the overall literacy rates lower than that of the national average. Among the total tribal literates, 33.6 per cent are either without any educational level or have attained education below primary level. The proportions of literates who have attained education up to primary level and middle level are 28.6 percent & 17.7 per cent respectively.

Persons educated up to matric / secondary / higher secondary constitute 16.5 percent. This implies that every 6th tribal literate is amatriculate. Graduates and above are 3.5 per cent while non-technical & technical diploma holders constitute a negligible 0.1 per cent only. While Kharia, Oraon and Ho have the highest proportion of matriculates i.e.every 5th literates of these tribes are matriculates closely followed by Munda who have every 6th literate a matriculate.

Kharwar have the lowest percentage of matriculates, preceded by Bhumij, Lohra and Santhal. While Oraon and Kharia have the highest percentage of graduates, Bhumij have the lowest proportion of degree holders, preceded by Kharwar, Lohra and Santhal. The data show that the proportion of tribal literates decline sharply in higher level of education as the percentage of students after matriculation drops down to almostone third in higher secondary level. Out of the total 19.8 lakh tribal children in the age group 5 –14 years, only 8.5 lakh children have been attending school constituting 43.1 per cent. Alarmingly, as many as 11.3 lakh (56.9 per cent) children in the corresponding age group have not been going to school. The Statement below shows that among the major STs, Oraon, Kharia and Munda have more than 50 per cent school going children whereas Santhal, Ho, Lohra have 36–47 per cent children attending school.

Tribal festivals in Jharkhand

Sarhul

People worshiping under holy sarna tree on the occasion of sarhul in outskirts of Ranchi, Jharkhand.

Sarhul is spring festival celebrated during spring season when the Saal trees get new flowers on their branches. It is a worship of the village deity who is considered to be the protector of the tribes. People sing and dance a lot when the new flowers appear. The deities are worshiped with saal flowers. The village priest or Pahan fasts for a couple of days. In the early morning he takes a bath and puts on new a dhoti made of virgin cotton (kachha dhaga). The previous evening, the Pahan takes three new earthen pots and fills them with fresh water; the next morning he observes these earthen pots and water level inside. If the water level decreases he predicts that there would be famine or less rain, and if the water level is normal, that is the signal of a good rain. Before pooja starts, the wife of the Pahan washes his feet and gets blessings from him. At the pooja, Pahan offers three young roosters of different colors to one for the almighty god — the Singbonga or Dharmesh, as the Mundas, Ho and Oraons respectively address Him; another for the village deities; and the third for the ancestors. During this pooja villagers surround the Sarna place. Traditional drum — Dhol, Nagara and Turhi — players keep drumming and playing along with Pahan chanting prayers to deities. When pooja is finished, boys carry Pahan on their shoulders and girls dancing ahead take him to his house where his wife welcomes him by washing his feet. Then Pahan offers Saal flowers to his wife and villagers. These flowers represent the brotherhood and friendship among villagers and Pahan the priest, distributes saal flowers to every villager. He also puts saals flowers on every house's roof which is called "phool khonsi". At the same time Prasad, a rice made beer called Handia, is distributed among the villagers. And the whole village celebrates with singing and dancing this festival of Sarhul. It goes on for weeks in this region of Chhotanagpur. In Kolhan region it is called "Baa Porob" meaning Flower Festival. It is the festival of the great happiness.

Mage Porob

Mage Porob is the principal festival celebrated among the Ho people of eastern India, and is also celebrated by the Munda people, though followers of Birsa Dharam, a new religionbased on traditional Munda spirituality and religion, do not celebrate Mage Porob, despite the fact that they celebrate other traditional Munda festivals. It is also not celebrated by any other Munda-speaking peoples, and is much less prominent to the Mundas than to the Hos. It is held in the month of Magha in honor of the deity Singbonga who, in the Ho creation myth, created *Luku Kola*, the first man on Earth. It was first described in 1912 by Indian anthropologist Rai Bahadur Sarat Chandra Roy in his *The Mundas and their Country*.

Jawa

At the same time, the unmarried tribal girls celebrate the Jin awa festival, which has its own kind of songs and dance.

This is held mainly for the expectation of good fertility and better household. The unmarried girls decorate a small basket with germinating seeds. It is believed that the worship for good germination of the grains would increase the fertility. The girls offer green melons to the Karam deity as a symbol of 'son' which reveals the primitive expectation of human being (i.e., grains and children). The entire tribal area of Jharkhand becomes tipsy during this time.

Hal Punhya

Hal punhya is a festival which begins with the fall of winter. The first day of Magh month, known as "Akhain Jatra" or "Hal Punhya", considered as the beginning of ploughing. The farmers, to symbolize this auspicious morning plough two and half circles of their agricultural land this day is also considered as the symbol of good fortune.

Bhagta Parab

This festival comes to between the period of spring and summer. Among the tribal people of Jharkhand, Bhagta Parab is best known as the worship of Budha Baba. People fast during the day and carry the bathing Pahan the priest, to the tribal mandir called Sarana Mandir.

The Pahan sometimes called Laya, gets out of the pond, the devotees make a chain, locking their thighs with each other and come forward to offer their bare chest to Laya for walk over. After worship in the evening, devotees take part in dynamic and vigorous Chhau dance with lots of gymnastic actions and masks. The next day is full of primitive sports of bravery. The devotees pierce hooks on skin and get tied at one end of a long horizontal wooden pole, which is hanging on the top of a vertical Shal wood pole. The height goes up to 40 feet. The other end of the pole which is connected with a rope, pulled around the pole by the people and the tied devotee display the breath-taking dance in the sky. This festivals is more popular in the Tamar region of Jharkhand.

Tribal artwork

- Chhou mask - Chhou is a type of dance done with colourful masks. The masks are made of paper mache in Singhbhum and purulia district of Jharkhand and west Bengal respectively. Paper mache of Saraikela and Charinda are famous for Chhou dance. Some times it appears similar to the masks used in kerla in Kathakali.
- Tribal woodwork - Jharkhand is full of good quality saal forest and hence wooden artwork in the "should" of tribals. The wood is used for cooking, housing, farming, fishing etc. The tribal artists of some villages have explored their creativity in art, like beautifully decorative door panels, toys, boxes, and other household articles.
- Tribal Painting - The painting is mainly a source of livelihood for Santhal tribe in Jharkhand and practiced in the region of Santhal Pragana and nearby areas.
- Tribal Bamboo Artwork - The bamboo found in this area are different from bamboo of Southeast Asia. There is tourist place, Netarhat, which means a Bazaar of Bamboo. These bamboos are thin, and strong and flexible. The tribal people use bamboo for making baskets, hunting & fishing equipments. Specially the bamboo made fishing cage is very attractive.
- Tribal Pottery - Tribal pottery is a part of tribals but still no specific working style observed.
- Tribal jewellery - The tribal people particularly like jewellery. They use metallic ornaments made of gold, silver, brass, copper for their earrings, nose ring, bracelets, bangles etc.
- Godna - Tribals use ornaments a lots but the spiritual concept of ornament is very different. They believe that all ornaments are human made and are mortal. Therefore, they invented tattoos as permanent ornament. Majority of tribal woman have tattoos called Godna, on their bodies. However, tribal man also use Godna.They believe that

Godna are the only ornament which goes with them after death also.

- Tribal weapons - Bow and arrow is the symbolic weapon of the tribals of this area. Apart from this they use iron made Axes and Doulies and Ghana (Big hammer).

Tribal religion: Sarna

Although, Hinduism is the predominant religion of the State (68.6 per cent), the Hindu tribes constitute 39.8 per cent only. As many as 45.1 per cent of the tribal population follow 'other religions and persuations'. Christian tribes are 14.5 per cent and less than half per cent (0.4 per cent) are Muslims. Among the major tribes, more than half of the total population (56.6 per cent) of nature worshipping Santals are 'Bedins' who also worship bongas. Oraon and Munda have more than 50 per cent of population follow 'other religions and persuasions' followed by Christianity. Ho tribe has the highest proportion (91per cent) of persons professing 'other religions and persuations'.*

Sarna religion/Sarna Dharam (regarded by tribals as Sari Dharam, that means True Religion) is religion of tribals of India. They have their own worship place called "SARNA ASTHAL/JAHER". They have also religious flag called "SARNA JHANDA". Which can be seen more in Ranchi District. In Ranchi the capital of jharkhand, there are "SARNA ASTHAL". In SARHUL festival every Oraon gather in Ranchi with a great Rally. In this time "SARNA JHANDA" can be seen every where in Ranchi. Some tribe followed Sarna Dharam, where Sarna means sacred grove. Their religion is based on the oral traditions passed from generation-to-generation. The religion is deeply ingrained in their culture and traditions, respecting the superiority of our natural world and its power. It strongly believes in one God, the Supreme Being, the Great Spirit, the Great One, the Creator, the Mighty Spirit, the one who rules over the entire universe, known as Dharmesh. They strongly believe in Lord Dharmesh's appearance in Sal trees.

According to their philosophy, the lord Dharmesh is the most powerful and most important deity. He is responsible for the creation of our universe including our ancestors besides acting as our protector. In fact, the whole world (Universe) is regulated by a superpower that is Dharmesh in Kurukh which simply means the almighty, he is also called Mahaedeo. The great one Dharmesh's purity demands that he be offered sacrifices only of things that are white. Hence he is given sacrifices of white goats, white fowls, white gulainchi flowers, white cloth, sugar, milk, etc. White is the sacred colour of Oraon tribe, in fact it is true for most adivasi.

Among the many important deities, the Chala-pacho Devi (Sarna Devi) is among the most important and most respected deity. The Gram Devi Chala-Pachho is a caring Old age lady with beautifully flowing white hair. It is believed that the Sal tree is the holy abode of the Sarna Devi, the mother goddess that protects and nurtures the Oraon tribe and others. On the occasion of Sarhul festival, the Pahan conducts special puja of the Devi. According to Sarna Dharam, the Devi lives in the wooden soop of Pahan kept at Chala-Kutti place, the auspicious place at Pahan's home. At Kutti place, one stick made up of Saal wood or Bamboo Wood is fixed on the ground, on this respected wooden soop called Sarna-Soop, the Sarna-Devi resides.

Tribals perform rituals under the Sal trees at a place called 'Sarna Sthal', it is also known as 'Jaher' (sacred grove); it resembles a small forest patch. In Oraons' villages, one can easily find the sacred religious place the 'Sarna Sthal' that has holy Sal trees and other trees planted at the site. Sometimes the Jaher are located inside the nearby forest area and not in the village.

This Sarna Sthal (Jaher) is a common religious place for the whole village and almost all the important socio-religious ceremonies of the village take place at this place only. These ceremonies are performed by the whole village community at a public gathering with the active participation of village priests known as 'Pahan'. The chief assistant of village priest is called 'Pujaar' or 'Panbhara'.

The tribals have their own way of conscience, faith and belief. Basically, they believe in the super natural spirit called the Singbonga.

According to the belief of the Santhal community, the world is inhabited by spiritual beings of different kinds; and the Santhals consider themselves as living and doing everything in close association with these supernatural beings. They perform rituals under the Sal trees at a place called "Jaher" (sacred grove). Often the Jaher can be found in the forests. They believe in Bonga's appearance in Sal trees and have named their religion "Sarna."

The genesis of the Sarna religion is interesting. According to the mythology of the Santhal community, the Santhal tribals had gone to the forest for hunting and they started the discussion about their 'Creator and Savior' while they were resting under a tree.

They questioned themselves that who is their God? Whether the Sun, the Wind or the Cloud? Finally, they came to a conclusion that they would leave an arrow in the sky and wherever the arrow would target that will be the God's house. They left an arrow in the sky; it fell down under a Sal tree. They started worshiping the tree and named their religion as "Sarna" because it is derived from a Sal tree. Thus, Sarna religion came into existence. There are priests and an assistant priests called "Naikey" and "Kudam Naike" in every Santhal village.

Name of one Sarna Union

All India Sarna Dhorom, at Jhoradi Odisha in the district of Mayurbhanj. It was from this union that as many procession, demonstration with their drums and equipment like TUMDH, TAMAK, GHURI, CHORCHURI, AAH, SAR, KHANDA,

TARWALE etc. held in the various part of the country like Odisha, Jharkhand, West Bengal, Madhya Pradesh and in many other places, their aims and objective was to raise the audible voice in ears of State and Central Government so that they are being protected from extinct and their laws and religious are being valued by Government and people of India as other religious.It has its Law and order made by its cabinet committee and it is being followed by all Sarnaism .

They too organize seminars, conferences to enhance their Laws and Order among all Sarnaism. There are many charitable trust to provide free medical treatment among the poor people, they too, run many schools and colleges in the mentioned state of India.

2

Culture and Society

CULTURE

Cuisine

Staple food of Jharkhand are rice, dal, vegetable and tubers. Spices are sparingly used in cuisine. Famous dishes include Chirka roti, Malpua, Pittha, Dhuska, Arsa roti, Dudhauri, Litti Chokha and Panipuri (Gupchup).Rugra is a unique type of mushroom that is grown extensively in Jharkhand and harvested during the rainy months. It has a hardened, white, edible shell and a softer dark colored centre. Bamboo shoots are also used as vegetable.

Local alcoholic drinks include rice beer, originally known as Handi or Handia , named after the vessel handi(earthen pot) used to make it. Handiya is culturally associated with native i.e. Sadans and Tribal, this drink consumed by both men and women, on social occasions like marriage and other festivals. Another common liquor is called *Mahua daru*, made from flowers of the "Mahua" tree (Madhuca longifolia).

Folk Music and Dance

There are several Folk dance in Jharkhand such as: Jhumair, Mardana Jhumair, Janani Jhumair, Domkach, Lahasua, Vinsariya, Jhumta, Fagua, Painki and Chhau. The musical instruments used in folk song and dance are Mandar, Dholki, Bansi, Nagara, Dhak, Shehnai, Khartal, Narsinga etc.

Festivals

Major local festival of Jharkhand are Karam, Jitia, Nawakhani, Sohrai/Bandna/Diwali, Phagua, Tussu, Vaha, Sarhul and Dussehra etc.

Paintings

Sahrai Painting perfermed during Sohrai festival. Various design are painted in Courtyard and wall.

Tattoo

The tattoo making tradition of Godna is essential part of local tradition.

Cinema

Jharkand produce many flims in regional and Tribal languages including Nagpuri, Khortha, Santali, Ho and Kurukh etc.

CULTURE OF JHARKHAND

Culture of Jharkhand refers to the culture of Indian state of Jharkhand, located in East India and surrounded by states of Bihar West Bengal, Uttar Pradesh, Chhatisgarh, and Odisha. The culture of Jharkhand is diverse with many languages, ethnic groups, traditions and festivals.

Languages

Hindi is official language of Jharkhand. There are many regional and tribal languages in Jharkhand.

The regional languages belongs to the Indo-Aryan branch in Jharkhand are Khortha, Nagpuri, Kurmali, Maithili, Bengali and Odia. The languages belongs to the Austroasiatic branch are Mundari, Santali and Ho. The languages belongs to the dravidian family are Kurukh and Malto.

Cuisine

The staple foods in Jharkhand are rice, dal, vegetables and tubers. Some dishes include Chirka roti, Pittha, Malpua, Dhuska, Arsa roti, and Litti Chokha. Rugra, a type of mushroom, and bamboo shoots are also used as vegetables. The leaf of Munga tree(Moringa oleifera) and Koinar tree(Bauhinia variegata) are used as leafy vegetable or Saag.

Local alcoholic drinks are Handia a rice beer and *Mahua daru*, made from flowers of the Mahua tree.

Festivals

Karam

Karam is major native festival of Jharkhand. It celebrated on the 11th day of a full moon of Bhado month, by Sadan (Khortha, Nagpuri, Kurmali speaking ethinic group) and tribal(Munda, Santal and Kurukh) people of Jharkhand.In this festival, people bring branches of Karam tree to the village. The branches then placed on the ground. The branches are washed with milk and handia. The branches are then decorated with garlands, curd, rice, flowers and grains.

Jitia

During the festival of Jitia, mothers fast for the well being of their children. It celebrated from the seventh to ninth lunar day of Krishna-Paksha in Ashwin month.

Nawakhani

Nawakhani is important festival of Jharkhand. During the festival, grains are eaten following the harvest.

Sohrai/Bandna

Sohrai is cattle festival of Jharkhand. It celebrated during the Amavasya of Kartik month. It coincides with Diwali festival. People fast throughout the day, and bathe cattle. In the evening, sacrifices are offered to the cattle deity.

Phaguwa

Phaguwa or Holi is the spring festival which falls in the month of Phalgun.

Sarna

Sarna festival celebreted in the month of Jyestha. In this festival, villager offer sacrifice to their respective village deity or Gramdev in Sacred grove to protect the village from disease and evil spirit.

Other festivals

Other festival are Tussu, Vaha, Sarhul and Dussehra etc.

Folk Dance

There are several folk dances in Jharkhand, inclining Jhumair, Mardana Jhumair, Janani Jhumair, Domkach, Lahasua, Vinsariya, Jhumta, Fagua, Painki and Chhau. The musical instruments used in include Mandar, Dholki, Bansi, Nagara, Dhak, Shehnai, Khartal, and Narsinga, among others.

- Jhumair: Jhumair is popular folk dance of Jharkhand. It perfermed during harvest season and festivals. The musical instruments used in include Mandar, Dhol, Bansi, Nagara, Dhak, Shehnai and Khartal. People hold hand and dance in circle. There are varieties of Jhumair dance such as Khortha Jhumair, Nagpuri Jhumair and Kurmali Jhumair. Nagpuri Jhumair also have Mardana Jhumair and Janani Jhumair.
- Domkach: Domkach dance performed by family of bridegroom on the occasion of marriage. The song are satrical. There are many songs of domkach such as ek haria, dohri, adh ratia, bihanwa.
- Painki: Painki is Nagpuri martial dance. It is perfermed by men. Men wear ghungroo, dance holding sword and shield accompanied by music of instruments Nagara, Dhak and Shehnai.

- Chhau dance: Chhau dance is a semi classical dance with martial, tribal and follk tradition. Seraikella Chhau is found in Seraikella district of Jharkhand.
- Mundari dance: Munda tribe performed this dance during harvest season and festivals.
- Santali dance: Santal tribe performed it during harvest season and festivals.

Paintings

Sahrai painting is performed during the Sohrai festival. Various design are painted in courtyards and on walls.

Tattoo

The local tattoo tradition of Godna is an essential part of local tradition.

Cinema

Jharkand produces many films in regional languages, including Nagpuri, Khortha, Santali, Ho and Kurukh etc. The first feature film of Jharkhand was *Aakarant* made under the banner of drishyantar international, 1988. The first Nagpuri flim was *Sona Kar Nagpur* (1994) produced and directed by Dhananjay Nath Tiwari.

CUISINE OF JHARKHAND

Jharkhand cuisine encompasses the cuisine of the Indian state of Jharkhand.

Staple food of Jharkhand are rice, dal, vegetable and tubers. Common meals often consist of vegetables that are cooked in various ways, such as curried, fried, roasted and boiled.

Traditional dishes of Jharkhand may not be available at restaurants. However, on a visit to a local village, one can get a chance to taste such exotic foods. Some dish preparations may be mild with a low oil and spice content, although pickles and festive dishes may have such characteristics.

Foods and dishes

- Chirka roti: It is popular roti in Jharkhand prepared using rice flour.
- Pittha: Pittha is made by boild rice flour. It is prepared during festivals.
- Malpua: It is dish in Jharkhand which prepared in Holi festival.
- Arsa Roti: It is a sweet dish prepared during festivals. Rice flour and sugar or jaggey used in preparation.
- Dhuska: A common food in Jharkhand is *dhuska*, which are deep fried rice flour pancakes that may be served with gram curry and potato.
- Litti Chokha: Bihari Cuisine also famous in the State.
- Tilkut: It is a sweet prepared with "pounded sesame-seed cookies made with jaggery batter or melted sugar."
- Thekua: It is a sweet prepared with whole-meal flour, jaggery and ghee, the latter of which is a type of clarified butter. It is prepared and consumed during the *Chhath* festival, which celebrates the Sun God.
- Sattu: Sattu is a common dish prepared with roasted chickpea flour that is prepared in various manners.
- Meat salaan: A popular meat dish which consists of lamb curry and diced potato that is spiced with *garam masala*.
- Spicy chicken: It is another common meat dish.
- Mushroom: *Gugra* and *Puttu* are a type of edible mushroom grows during monsoon season which used for vegetable.
- Bamboo shoot: Bamboo shoots are used as vegetable in Jharkhand.
- Red ant chutney: It is dish made of mashed red ants and their eggs.

Leaf-based dish

- Munga saag: Munga tree(Moringa oleifera) is an important tree in Jharkhand. It's leaf, flower and fruit used as vegetable. It's leaf are used as leafy vegetable or Saag.

- Koinar Saag: The leaf of Koinar tree(Bauhinia variegata) used as vegetable.

Alcoholic beverage

- Handia: Handia or Handi is common rice beer in Jharkhand. people drink it in festivals and Marriage.
- Mahua daru: It is alcoholic beverage in Jharkhand which prepared using flower of Mahaua tree(Madhuca longifolia).

Food security

The twenty-four districts of Jharkhand receive supplemental food security supplies as per the National Food Security Act, 2013 of India. In the past, food supplies were distributed to the districts in phases, which some have criticized as problematic. In June 2015, Ram Vilas Paswan, the Minister of Consumer Affairs, Food and Public Distribution for the government of India stated a preference toward the Food Security Act to be implemented all at once, rather than in phases. In this manner, Paswan stated a preference for distributions to be completed in entirety by September 1, 2015.

FOLK DANCES OF JHARKHAND

Folk dances of Jharkhand represent its vibrant culture and tradition. There are various folk dance in the state of Jharkhand which are performed during harvest season, festival and social gatherings. Some folk and tribal dances in Jharkhand are Jhumair, Mardana Jhumair, Janani Jhumair, Domkach, Lahasua, Jhumta, Fagua, Painki, Chhau, and Santali.

Folk dance

Folk dance performed by various community in harvest season, Marriage and festival.

Jhumair

Jhumair is popular folk dance of Jharkhand. It performed during harvest season and festivals. Musical Instruments used are Mandar, Dhol, Nagara, Dhak, Bansi Shehnai.

Mardana Jhumair

Mardani Jhumair is Nagpuri folk dance performed by men. Men war ghungroo, hold sword and dance in circle . Musical instruments used are Nagara, dhak and Shehnai.

Janani Jhumair

Janani Jhumair is Nagpuri folk dance performed by women.

Domkach

Domkach is a folk dance performed by women in family of bridegroom during marriage. The lyrics of the song are satirical. There are different songs of domkach such as ek haria, dohri, adh ratia, bihanwa.

Lahasua

Lahasua is a Nagpuri folk dance performed by both men and women The musical instruments used are Mandar, Dhol and Bansi.

Painki

Painki is Nagpuri ceremonial martial dance. It is performed by men. Men wear ghungroo, dance holding sword and shield. Music instruments used are Nagara, Dhak and Shehnai.

Chhau dance

Chhau dance is a semi classical Indian dance with martial, tribal and folk tradition. Seraikella Chhau is found in Seraikella district of Jharkhand.

Tribal folk dance

Tribal folk dance performed by a particular tribe which have its own song and rhythm.

Mundari dance

Munda tribe have its own dance which performed during

harvest season and festival accompanied by musical Instrument Madal, Nagara and Bansi.

Santali dance

Santal tribe have its own unique dance. They performed it during harvest season and festival accompanied by music of Instrument such as Madal and Nagara.

JHARKHAND : REPOSITORY OF ONE OF INDIA'S RICHEST ETHNIC CULTURES

The cultural mosaic of Jharkhand was dreamt about, shaped and polished by generations of communities, which have inhabited this land since time immemorial. From the legendary Asurs and Santhals, to the Banjara, Bihor, Chero, Gond, Ho, Khond, Lohra, Mai Pahariya, Munda, Oraon, Kol or Kawar-over thirty-two tribal groups (28 % of the total population of the state), have left their impression on the culture of the region. And with them, were the cross-cultural influences of local non-tribal communities and successive waves of Buddhism and Jainism, Mughal rule and the reign of the Hindu emperors of Bengal. Art historians ascribe the 'oldest cave paintings' in India, the "scroll paintings" to a Jharkhand tribe known as the Shabars, who today live on the edge of extinction. It is an established fact that Stone Age tools discovered in Hazaribagh district and axes and spearheads found in the Chaibasa area, are remnants of a civilization dating back a few thousand years. 10,000 to 30,000 years old rock paintings, paintings in huge caves in the Sati hills and other indicators of ancient, even pre-historic, human settlements are found in profusion.

Living Rhythms

Every ethnic community has the blood of tribal memory circling their hearts. Today the Adivasis of Jharkhand are coming back, not to the despair that has marked their recent history, but to the strong sounds of drums, flutes, cymbals and voices raised in song. When the tribes of Jharkhand gather to celebrate a very special occasion, whether at home or in village society, they make music and dance to its rhythm. Maybe it makes them happy because it brings that long memory back, into the framework of real life. It does not matter whether you understand the language or the lyrics of the song that the; sing - ekhariya damckach, orjapi, jhumar, fagua, veer seren, jhika, philsanjha, adhratiya or bhinsariya, doad, asadi, jhumti, or dhuria or other important folk-songs - you will recognize that they yearn to carry ancient memory and culture into their lives today. Percussion, many kinds of percussion, along with a variety of musical instruments are used by Jharkhand tribes to accompany their singing and dancing. The Nagara, made of wood and stretched animal hide played with drumsticks. Interestingly nagaras sound the best in summers, in winter they lose their vibrant beat. The cylindrical Mandar, played by hand. Dhak, dhamsa, damana, Madan bhewri, ananad lahari, tuila, vyang, ar-bansi, shankh, karha, tasa, thala, ghanta, kadri and gupi jantra are some quaint instruments played.

Dance forms echo warrior-like movements of battles fought long ago, for the men. Observations of animal and bird behaviour were also blended into the dancing, sometimes light and airy, sometimes heavy and solemn, as the mood demands. Everyday activities of womenfolk -working in the fields, in the forests, in their homes, all reflect themselves in dance forms like the timeless Chhau, which requires agility, suppleness, skilful hand movements. The Seraikela school of Chhau is held during the Sun Festival. It is influenced by the principles of Bharatiya Natya Shastra but the theme is based on folk-lore, nature and mythology. The choreograph follows Odissi in composition and execution. Other well-known dances of tribal communities in Jharkhand include festive dancing such as - Sarhul /Baha, where sal and mohua flowers are used ceremonially; the Dansai & Sorhai where the youth sing and dance through the night of karam; Maghi Puja, an important festival of the Munda tribe; Sarhul in which 'shalai' the flower of the sal tree is offered to the gods, with the flower as a symbol of brotherhood; Tusu, the harvest festival, celebrated mainly by unmarried girls. A conopy is ade of light wood and covered with thin tissue paper. The pyramidal shaped structure, edged with tinsel and decorated with painted/printed images of local deities (sometimes even film stars), is carried by village woman-chanting songs along the way-to the nearest water resource and immersed in it. Bazra Puja, when Bazra or 'millet' is ready for harvesting; and the Bhagta Parab or the worship of Budha Baba.

Most of the folk dance around Jharkhand is accompanied by traditional music played by the musicians using some traditional musical equipment. Some of the very famous Jharkhand dances are as follows:

Paika is one of the very famous dance forms of Jharkhand. In fact, it is a dance form where martial arts are mixed with some other dance steps. This is why the dance form is only performed by the male members of the society. Paika of Jharkhand is a very interesting dance form of the region. It offers a thrilling entertainment to your eyes as the men risk their lives to perform it. The dancers have to handle a sword in one hand and the shield in other. For protection, they are dressed with safety chest plates and head wears and bells are tied on their ankles. in Jharkhand is accompanied by the melodious music of Narsingha, Shahnai, Bheir and the Dhak and Nagara drums. This folk dance of Jharkhand is performed for welcoming guests during various functions. The whole ambience during the performance of this dance form is very charming. The dancers wearing their colorful robes along with the local tribes create fascinating scenery. The dance adds more glaze to the festivities.

Chhau is one of the finest folk dances of Chhota Nagpur Plateau region. The folk dance is performed in various states that lie in this region such as West Bengal, Bihar, Orissa and Jharkhand. The word Chhau is derived from the Sanskrit word Chhaya which implies shade, image, or mask. Chhau of Jharkhand is a very beautiful dance form where the dancers cover their faces during the dance with a mask and it is this mask that attracts your attention towards the dance. Chhau is different from classical dance because in the latter dance form facial expressions are must, whereas in Chhau, it is the body movements including the neck and head gesture. In Chhau, the dancers use the mask and their body gestures to convey the stories. A commentator stands aside who not only narrates the whole story with dialogues but also sings the songs. During Chhau in Jharkhand, music is played using various instruments such as Nagara, Jhanj, Mohuri, Turi, Clude Dhol, Dhumsa, Flute, Bheri and Conch shells.

Over the years, this folk dance of Jharkhand has been classified into various forms but the most authentic and original version of the dance is available only in Jharkhand. The melodious music and the colorful dancers with their brilliant dancing skills intoxicate you so much that you do not feel like leaving the place before its completion. So if you like dancing and are always open to learn, then the best place to learn would be in Jhrakhand where the original version is performed. Some of the very famous stories that have been performed through Chhau in Jharkhand are Ramayana and Mahabharata.

Santhal is a very popular folk dance of Jharkhand. It is a group dance performed by Santhal tribes of Jharkhand. This dance was performed by the Santhal tribes during all special festivals and occasions. This dance not only reveals the culture or traditions of the local tribes but also showcases the strength of unity. The main attraction of the dance in Jharkhand are the colorful costumes worn by the tribal people. The typical garments worn by men during the Santhal are dhoti and a turban but the main attraction is their body decoration with various species of flora. Since the Santhal are believed to be close to nature, they use natural things such as leaves, branches and flowers to do their make-up and design their clothes.

If you wish to witness the fun and frolic of Santhal dance at Jharkhand then do visit it during the spring season for it is during this season that the Santhals celebrate the spring festival where they perform the folk dance. The colorful environment of the festival is made more charming and attractive by the musicians who play the music on various folk instruments such as cymbals, pipes, flutes and drums. Moreover, the singers also put the right chord with the rhythm. After, the Bamboo folk dance of Assam and Mizoram, it is the Santhal dance of Jharkhand which is very popular among the tourists of north eastern region. Moreover, the Santhal dance would also help you in exploring the life style and culture of the Santhals.

Karma is a very popular folk dance of India. Though the folk dance is performed in other states such as Bihar, Madhya Pradesh and Chhattisgarh, it can be enjoyed the best in Jharkhand. The folk dance is performed in the month of August during the Karma festival.This folk dance of Jharkhand has derived its name from a tree named Karma which is considered sacred because people believe that it brings good luck and prosperity. Hence the Karma festival is nothing but a celebration for the plantation of this tree. Karma at Jharkhand seeks the participation of both men and women. The festival starts with the plantation of trees after which the dancers get into a circle and dance with their hands around each other's waists. While dancing, they pass on the branch of the tree to each other. After the branch of Karma gets a complete circle, it is washed with milk and rice. It is the belief of the local tribes that after these rituals, the branch should not touch the earth. After this, once again the branch is raised in between the dancers. During the Karma of Jharkhand, the men leap forward with the rapid roll of the drums whereas the women bend down with their feet moving to and fro with the beats of the music. The dance of Karma in Jharkhand is accompanied by the melodious music of folk music instruments such as Jhumki, Thumki, Chhalla and Payri. Various forms of Karma are performed in various regions. The two most popular forms of Karma in Jharkhand are Lahsua and Khare. This dance in Jharkand is performed mainly by Baigas and Gonds.

Art, Craft & Living

Jharkhand is full of surprises. Archeaologists have unearthed pre-Harappan pottery, and pre-historic cave paintings and rock-art, that hint at ancient, cultured civilizations inhabiting these parts. Who exactly were the original settlers of Jharkhand? We will never truly know. But one look at the intricate woodwork, the pitkar paintings, tribal ornaments, stone carvings, dolls and figurines, masks and baskets, will tell you how deep into time these manifestations of culture go, how the well-spring of creativity continues to recharge the spirit of the tribes and the state itself.Among the most delicate, fragile, beautiful ands threatened indigenous traditions of India are for example, the Kohvar and Sohrai paintings, which are sacred, secular and relevant to a woman's world. This is the art practiced exclusively by married women, during weddings and at harvest time, and the skill and the information is handed down to younger females of the clan.Comb-cut or finger-painted, Kohvar art celebrates marriage, and the wall-painted Sohrai, bumper crops. Elaborate design motifs, animal and plant forms, fertility motifs are abundant and often echo ancient cave art found in the surrounds. The colours used are all natural - neutral earth shades, red oxide from stone, red ochre, kaolin white, manganese black earth etc.. Blue and green are aberrant colours and do not feature prominently.

Jharkhand is known for its wood work, bamboo works, pitkar paintings, tribal ornaments and stone carving. The beautifully carved wood products and bamboo products show the craftsmanship of the people. Lack of promotion and marketing for these products has mostly resulted in extinction of some crafts like paitkar paintings and stone carvings. Wood Craft: Once a dense forest area, Jharkhand with the abundance of wood, resulted in the use this for creating variety of wood articles for household requirements. Bamboo: The bamboos found in the Jharkhand forest are thin but flexible and strong. Using these, the artisans of Jharkhand produce different artifacts like basket, haunting and fishing equipment.The people here are to be much involved into artistic approaches in whatever they work, to name some of the fame arts in this region could be Oraon Bhitichitra , Santhali Bhitichitra and Jado Patiya are the styles of paintings that still exist.

Distinctive Traditions

Each sub-caste and tribal grouping Jharkhand has a unique tradition to uphold.

Oraon comb-cut paintings can be traced back to ancient times. Images of cattle, feeding troughs, papyrus, birds, fish, plants, circled lotus, zigzag, square,opposing triangle geometric forms, arches in series - are common. Floral art forms are used during harvest time.

Ganju art forms are characterized by images of animals, wild and domesticated, and plant forms. Large murals of animals, birds, and floral exotica, decorate homes. Endangered animals are often depicted in picture-story tradition.

Prajapati, Rana &Teli the three sub-castes decorate their homes with plant and animal fertility forms, using both finer painting and comb cutting techniques. The 'prajapati' style uses filigree work, with emphasis on zoomorphic plants representations and Pashupati (Siva) the God of Animals, and floral motifs filled with colour.

Kurmi an unique style of 'sohrai', where drawing outlines are scratched onto the surface of a wall with nails and a wooden compass is used to etch the segmented lotus. Pashupati or Lord Shiva is depicted as a horned deity on the back of a bull. Red, black and white lines are drawn in pairs on either side to represent the ashes of ancestors. The Kurmis of Bhehwara use glyptic art to represent plants on the walls and floors of their homes.

Mundas use their fingers to paint in the soft, wet earth of their homes and use unique motifs like the rainbow snake and plant forms of deities. Lavender-gray coloured mud from rock-art sites next to Munda villages, are used with ochre mud as contrast colour.

Ghatwals use glyptic paintings of animals on their forest dwellings.

Turi who are a small community of basket-makers use predominantly floral and jungle-based motifs in natural earthy tones on the walls of their homes.

Birhor & Bhuiya use simple, strong, and authentic graphic forms like 'mandalas', painting with their fingers. Crescents, stars, yoni, rectangles with corner petals, ovals with flared lines and concentric circles, are common.

Manjhi Santhal - the striking warring figures painted in black on simple clay plaster walls are startling reminders that their origins probably had links with the Indus Valley civilization.

SOCIETY

SLADS—Singhbhum Legal Aids Society

Project Description: The project area of 50 villages is populated mostly by poor tribals and economically backward communities. For the 20 primary schools in the area, SLADS is the only high school, which we fund for 3 years. The school targets 70 girls and 80 boys.

Funding request of an existing high school over 3 years which draws children from the SALBONI area (50 villages, 20,000 population). The funding requested is for teaching staff salary/training, books for a library, apparatus for a laboratory, furniture, and administrative costs. The proposal requests roughly $9000 over this three year period.

Purpose/Goals: Strengthening the Secondary Education of the poor children in the tribal area.

(i) Improving the quantitative and qualitative development of the children in the school.

(ii) To promote the meaningful constructive secondary education in this area.

Organization Description: There are 20 primary schools in the area run by government funds, and the school currently run by S.L.A.D.S. is the only high school (secondary education) in the SALBONI area, covering a population of 20,000 in 50 villages. Due to a "serious financial crisis," the Bihar government is unable to fund secondary education and so the school is running with the efforst of volunteer teachers, local people, and social workers.

Project Type: Working with the Government (description)

Primary Focus: Other (description)

Area: Rural

Number of Children: 101

Boy/Girl Ratio: 1 : 1

Student/Teacher Ratio: 14 : 1

AID—Alternative for India Development

Project Description: Alternative for India Development (AID)

NFE schools for children employed in carpet-weaving industry.

Purpose/Goals: Basic education to about 400 young boys, aged 7-15, now sold into bonded labour (or virtual slavery) in the carpet manufacturing industry.

Providing recreation opportunity for carpet working children. Raising health status of carpet working children. Activation of existing formal schools of the government.

Raising of Parental awareness/education to 400 families of the working children on issues of literacy, child labour and health and local government programmes for prevention of child labour.

Enable the parents to utilise local government resources to improve their life.

Campaign against the use of child labour in the carpet industry and this will contribute to the gradual elimination of the system.

Organization Description: The mission of the organisation is to empower the grassroots communities to decide and determine their own needs and development by themselves with the active participation of the deprived communities.

Project Type: Non-Formal Educational Centres (description)

Primary Focus: Children who are working (description)

Area: Rural.

3

Government and Politics

GOVERNMENT AND ADMINISTRATION

The constitutional head of the government of Jharkhand is the governor, who is appointed by the President of India. The real executive power rests with the chief minister and the cabinet. The political party or the coalition of political parties having a majority in the Legislative Assembly forms the government.

The head of the bureaucracy of the state is the chief secretary. Under this position, is a hierarchy of officials drawn from the Indian Administrative Service, Indian Police Service, Indian Forest Service, and different wings of the state civil services. The judiciary is headed by the Chief Justice. Jharkhand has a High Court which has been functioning since 2000. All the branches of the government are located in the state capital, Ranchi.

Administrative districts

The state was formed with 18 districts that were formerly part of south Bihar. Some of these districts were reorganised to form 6 new districts, namely, Latehar, Saraikela Kharsawan, Jamtara, Sahebganj, Khunti and Ramgarh. At present, the state has 5 Divisions and 24 Districts. One interesting thing about Jharkhand is that all its districts, except Lohardaga and Khunti, share a border with a neighboring state.

GOVERNMENT OF JHARKHAND

The Government of Jharkhand also known as the State Government of Jharkhand, or locally as State Government, is the supreme governing authority of the Indian state of Jharkhand and its 24 districts. It consists of an executive, led by the Governor of Jharkhand, a judiciary and a legislative branch.

Like other states in India, the head of state of Jharkhand is the Governor, appointed by the President of India on the advice of the Central government. His or her post is largely ceremonial. The Chief Minister is the head of government and is vested with most of the executive powers. Ranchi is the capital of Jharkhand, and houses the Vidhan Sabha (Legislative Assembly) and the secretariat. The Jharkhand High Court, located in Ranchi, has jurisdiction over the whole state.

The present Legislative Assembly of Jharkhand is unicameral, consisting of 81 Member of the Legislative Assembly (M.L.A). Its term is 5 years, unless sooner dissolved.

ADMINISTRATIVE DIVISIONS OF JHARKHAND

Jharkhand state of India is divided into five Administrative Divisions namely *South Chhotanagpur*, *North Chhotanagpur*, *Kolhan*, *Palamu* and *Santhal Parganas*.

Background

Jharkhand state was created as 28th State of the Indian Union by the Bihar Re-organization Act on 15 November 2000. State was created due to its underdevelopment and social justice. Jharkhand has 5 neighborhood states e.g. Bihar on the North, Orissa on the South, Chhattisgarh and Uttar Pradesh on the west West Bengal on the East.

POLITY

One of the country's oldest, most wretched and most primitive lunatic asylums is located in Ranchi. As though that identity tag wasn't enough, now Jharkhand's politicians are infusing lunacy into Ranchi's politics.

It is in this eastern province that democratic fixers and political wheeler-dealers are making hay with or without the sun shining on them. And they are deliberately doing so because the present electoral arithmetic gives an Independent MLA the advantage of being on the top of a pile of mercenary politicians. Chief Minister Madhu Koda, country's first Independent Chief Minister, is ruling the state with a strategically thought-out policy of appeasement since September last year.

No, he is not a please-all populist. He is gratefully doling out favours to fellow-politicians who are helping him stay in power. Not that this strange and rather convenient policy of satisfying political co-passengers can last for long. Madhu Koda will soon run out of sops and carrots. Only then can the Jharkhand electorate, witnessing a farce in the name of governance, heave a sigh of relief and vote to bring in a new, stable administration.

You can grasp the extent of the damage being done to Jharkhand's polity when you comprehend the sheer absurdity of a particular political plot this writer is going to narrate. Bhanu Pratap Shahi surprised most, including himself, when he won the Bhawanathpur assembly seat in 2005. He was a nominee of Forward Bloc, a party that was never a part of Jharkhand's political geography.

The Forward Bloc itself was amazed to have won two seats. With the verdict quite fractured and, the composition of the legislature providing a dream playing-turf for smaller parties and Independents, Bhanu Pratap Shahi immediately understood his worth. He started his antics and was expelled from Forward Bloc, when much to the embarrassment of his party, he showed his inclination to join the Arjun Munda-led NDA government.

When four Independent MLAs, including Koda, switched sides and the fragile NDA government collapsed in a heap, Bhanu Pratap Shahi further increased his market value. Even Governor Syed Sibtey Razi, who had acquired a degree of notoriety for showing extraordinary partiality towards the UPA, recoiled at the thought of having to swear in Shahi as one of Koda's Cabinet ministers. Shahi had more than six cases pending against him including a murder charge.

But with the Koda government commanding only a wafer-thin majority and Shahi among the few who held the key to the survival of this equally brittle government, the murder accused insisted that he be made the twelfth and the final minister in the 82-member assembly. After the 91st amendment to the Indian Constitution, Jharkhand can have a maximum of 12 members in the ministerial council.

As luck would have it, it was around this crucial juncture in Shahi's political career that the law caught up with him. He had to be put behind bars. Believe it or not, his aging father, Hemender Pratap Shahi, who was nowhere in the picture and whose simple, pedestrian life was far removed from the glitzy corridors of power in Ranchi, was suddenly catapulted into the centrestage.

With his son counting time in jail, a shy and unprepared Hemender Pratap Shahi was sworn in as the state's health minister and held fort till Bhanu Pratap was bailed out. A defiant Madhu Koda said that it was the chief minister's prerogative to choose his ministers and anybody could occupy that post for a maximum period of six months without being elected. The senior Shahi quietly escaped from his position of pelf and power as soon as his son was released on bail.

And in the week when this compromised, handicapped government in Ranchi was going to complete five tumultuous months, the Supreme Court gave its verdict on the BSP MLAs who had shamelessly defected to strengthen the Mulayam Singh government in Lucknow more than three years ago. That defection had received the sanction of the then Speaker, Kesri Nath Tripathi even if it was staggered and even if there was actually more than one incident of defection.

The numbers soared and surpassed the permissible one-third mark long after the process of floor crossing began. We must remember here that in 2003, the 91st Amendment had not taken effect and defection was still adjudicated under the previous anti-defection law (52nd Constitutional Amendment), conceived and formulated during the late Prime Minister Rajiv Gandhi's tenure in 1985.

The 91st amendment is justifiably brutal towards the very idea of defection and split. If you want to split your parent party, you have to resign and contest again. A merger may be allowed only when two thirds of the total number of legislators of a particular party expresses its collective desire to cross over. The 91st amendment not only restricts the gifting of ministerial berths, but it also makes a bold attempt to terminate the cynical politics of Aya Rams and Gaya Rams.

The Supreme Court has held the defection of the first thirteen BSP MLAs illegal. The final decision on the fate of the others who had crossed over from their parent BSP has been left in the hands of the Speaker of the assembly. It means the court has made its disapproval of floor crossing absolutely clear. It also implies that the court has sought to maintain a distance from what it perceives to be legislative business and has left it to the Speaker to take necessary corrective action in the case of the other MLAs.

It is another matter that Mulayam Singh Yadav will not learn the necessary lesson from this judgment. Only a fortnight before this verdict, he had engineered the defection of fourteen MLAs including, at least eight, from a structured, disciplined party like the BJP during the floor-test that he took. In the coming elections, Uttar Pradesh is going to witness quadrangular contests. There is no guarantee even after the 91st Amendment that there will not be any horse-trading.

The 91st amendment is not a foolproof legal mechanism. It doesn't recognize splits but merger remains a way out for unscrupulous politicians in smaller assemblies. Jharkhand and Goa have been particularly vulnerable to the machinations of the power-hungry political sharks. Veerappa Moily's Administrative Reforms Commission has recently come up with the suggestion that even pre-poll alliances be treated with a degree of respect and rigidity and a party should not be allowed to walk out on its partner thereby threatening the coalition. But this is a meaningless and, arguably, even an undemocratic recommendation. What is needed at the moment is a legislation whereby Independents do not switch sides lured by money and power; and smaller parties don't get fragmented paving the way for unseemly mergers.

Till then, no amount of chastisement by the Supreme Court judges is going to change the course of Indian politics. And politicians like Madhu Koda will enjoy the licence to empty our treasuries and make the most of glaring systemic flaws.

POLITICAL MESS

It's the very first assembly election of the state but there is nothing to cheer about it. For, the state has inherited what it intended, at least in theory, to leave behind--the filthy politics of its parent state.

For, after five years of its creations, the election should have been fought on the issue of development and growth but unfortunately, underdevelopment is the often quoted term used for the state of Jharkhand.

And, if the incumbent BJP government failed to give a vision of development and a reason to hope, the choices available in the ongoing election do not give any vibes for development and progress either. Such, unfortunately, is the condition of the state polity as it goes for the polls for the very first time in its history.

Is this the reason, why so many people struggled so hard for years together, shedding their blood and sacrificing their lives?

Politicians are definitely to be blamed for so mercilessly butchering the hopes of the citizens and giving them a cause for dismay. They are also to be blamed for the growth of Naxalism in the state-a product of anarchy, which in turn is giving birth to chaos and lawlessness. Or, in other words, they are solely to be blamed creating a vicious cycle of underdevelopment and bedlam which will continue to dog the state for years together.

What else can be said, for naxalism was restricted to three districts five years back and today the their tentacles are firmly established in all the 18 districts of the state.

And, what can be expected of the leaders who were trained in the perverse political environment of Bihar polity. Some even believe that the condition of Jharkhand polity is worse than that of Bihar.

It is indeed very sad for the state, so rich in its natural resources-- having huge reserves of coal, copper, bauxite, mica, iron ore and ceramics. A state - possessing several industries dealing in steel, aluminum, cement, chemicals, jute, sugar, electrical equipment and fertilizer talking about under-development. It should rather have been giving competition to the states like Punjab and Karnataka.

But this is not to be, for so long as the caste and vote bank continue to dominate political scene crime and corruption is what it will produce in plenty. One cannot expect a vision and a mission for rapid economic progress, employment and a curb on naxalism from the government.

For, anything can be done to gain a seat of power here. Any type of alliance and any compromise can be made. People who are thirsty for each others blood can come together. Hug each other in front of the shutterbugs and praise each other. But, in the next election when the power equation so demand wash each others dirty linen in public... such is the lure for power... and such is the mess in the state of Jharkhand.

INDIAN POLITICAL PARTIES

Jharkhand Mukti Morcha (Jharkhand Liberation Front), a political party in Jharkhand, formed by Shibu Soren, Binod Bihari Mahato the marxist leader and trade unionist Comrade A. K. Roy of Marxist Coordination Committee became the chief ideologue. The party started as a mix of Marxism and tribal liberation (whom Roy termed as primitive communist society) Roy had propounded the theory of internal colony which was a new analysis in indian polity.

JHARKHAND VANANCHAL CONGRESS

Jharkhand Vananchal Congress, a political party in Jharkhand, India. The party is led by Samresh Singh. Singh is the only JVC member of the Jharkhand state legislative assembly.

MARXIST COORDINATION COMMITTEE

Marxist Coordination Committee, political party in Jharkhand, India. MCC is based in the coal mining region of Dhanbad.

Janwadi Kisan Sangram Samiti (Democratic Peasants Struggle Association) was formed after local communist leader A.K. Roy had been expelled from CPI(M). JKSS later converted into MCC. MCC is still led by A.K. Roy, who has been elected MP three times.

A.K. Roy was active in the Jharkhand movement, and co-founder of Jharkhand Mukti Morcha. As JMM developed into a political party, the relations soared.

In 1980 A.K. Roy (then MP) and K.S. Chatterjee (Member of Bihar Legislative Assembly) were arrested under the National Security Act. In total Roy has been jailed four times.

In 1998 the only Member of the Legislative Assembly of Bihar of MCC, Gurudas Chatterjee was murdered by the coal mafia. Chatterjee's son Arup Chatterjee took over his mandate after a by-poll.

VEER BIRSA DAL

Veer Birsa Dal, a splinter-group of the Jharkhand Party.

JHARKHAND PARTY

Jharkhand Party, a political party in India. The party was founded on March 5, 1949 at a large conference in Ranchi. Jaipal Singh was elected president and Idsen Deba general secretary. JKP grew out of the demand for a separate Jharkhand state.

The party fared well in the 1952 elections, and got three MPs elected.

In 1963 JKP merged with Indian National Congress. The merger was quite unpopular amongst the party ranks, and a variety of splinter groups, were formed, many of the claiming the name of JKP.

JHARKHAND MUKTI MORCHA

Jharkhand Mukti Morcha is a political party in India. It has a strength of 5 in the 14th Lok Sabha. 4 of its MPs are from Jharkhand. Shibu Soren is the president of JMM.

IMPACT OF CHRISTIANITY ON THE TRIBES

The present state of Jharkhand, which was carved out of Bihar in November 2000, is a part of Chhotanagpur plateau of Indian peninsula. Its complex social condition provided unique opportunity to the various socio-religious and anthropological groups for carrying out their intellectual pursuit in this most diverse cultural and linguistic area of central India.

But in the process of their academic romanticism the homogenous character of the tribal society got disturbed.

The social scientists, who believe in the history based on

Christian tradition, projected the tribes inhabited in this region as indigenous people. In fact the tribes of separate ethnic races settled here in course of their migration from different geographical regions of the subcontinent and as such the theory of their indigenous character became a debatable issue.

The respective dominant groups almost everywhere in the world have significantly used religion as tools to strengthen the mechanism for maintaining their hegemony in the society. Accordingly, colonial and imperialist forces of western world also used Christianity for furthering their colonial and cultural interest among the hapless multi-ethnic tribes settled in this region for centuries.

Advent of Christianity in Jharkhand dates back to 1845, when the first four Christian Missionaries from Germany established the Gossner Evangelical Lutheran Church in Ranchi, the present capital of Jharkhand State.

Gradually, the Churches of other denominations like Anglicans and Roman Catholic established their foothold in this region. These missionaries under the patronage of British colonial power gradually and steadily launched a cultural invasion on racially different tribes through proselytisation.

They successfully used religion as a mechanism to expand the hegemony of church among the 'indigenous' people of the area. Their zealous attempt to denunciate the socio-religious faith of the tribal people had the sole purpose to manipulate for the imposition of the Christian tradition of west in central India. In due course of time they succeeded to a considerable extent in imposing their moods, concepts and images on these 'indigenous tribes', though, it created a quagmire in the homogenous tribal society. Thus, contrary to the myth that the missionaries came to the area with caring and sharing philosophy - they were caring only for those who changed their socio-religious loyalty from SARANA (Sacred groves as place of worship by the local tribes) to GIRJA (Church).

Initially, the 'Bible came in conflict with sword'. At the initial stage even revolt by Birsa Munda (1890-1895) popularly known as Birsa Bhagwan among the tribal people of Jharkhand was an anti-Christian missionary movement, which was later projected as part of National Freedom Movement. Birsa even took exception to Christian Sunday as day for rest and prayer and substituted it with Thursday for the socio-religious congregation of his followers.

Though, in comparison to Hinduism, Christianity was a recent phenomenon in this region, the latter left a deep rooted and long-term impact on tribal mind and life. In fact the work of Christian missionaries not only covered the religious domain but it also influenced the socio-political life of the tribes settled here.

The land and forest, which belonged to the community, were the only source of their livelihood. But with commercialisation of these sources of their survival through introduction of Permanent Settlement Act by the then British Government, people lost their sources of livelihood. Taking advantage of their plight, the Christian missionaries intervened in the issue and helped the affected people to some extent by taking the British power into confidence. In the bargain they succeeded in converting a sizeable section of local inhabitants.

After establishing their foothold in the region Christian missionaries gradually monopolised the education as Church subject. With the patronage of British imperial power they succeeded in creating a dominant group within the tribal community through allurement and some philanthropic and social activities. Gradually they alienated the converts from the rest of their community members and forced them to accept the cultural tradition of the west at the cost of forgetting their respective socio-cultural tradition. In the process of such social transformation however, Christianity left a deep rooted negative impact on the life and mind of the tribal people, which may be described as under:

- Contrary to the collective outlook of tribal society, individual approach to life became prominent particularly among the converts, who represented the tribal elite.
- Community ownership of land and forest, which was the traditional means for subsistence was lost due to their commercialisation and barter economy was replaced by the market economy of the west.
- Practice of making social decision on the basis of consensus, which was a form of tribal democracy, was replaced by the concept of democracy with Christian tradition.
- Puritanism and conservatism of Christianity replaced animism, which was an underdeveloped form of liberal Hinduism.

By the time India attained Independence, the Christian missionaries successfully expanded their base among the different tribes of Chhotanagpur and also created church leaders from within the respective community. Switching over from socio-religious to politico religious mode for expanding their hegemony over the tribal people, Christian missionaries utilised the services of the converts to keep their community members away from their emotional integration with rest of the population of the country.

These leaders, who became the privileged group due to their education in western pattern subsequently, emerged as a viable force to guide the political movement of tribal people for a separate tribal land of Jharkhand. It may be worthwhile to mention that almost all the leaders of Jharkhand party, which emerged as a political outfit of the tribals in 1949, were Christians.

Unfortunately, the political dispensation of the country in post-colonial India never tried to understand the socio-cultural condition of the different ethnic groups particularly the tribals and allowed them to play in the hands of the alien forces responsible for the protracted unrest in the region. Taking advantage of the situation, Christian missionaries made concerted efforts to keep the tribals alienated from the mainstream polity of the country. However, heavy influx of non-tribal population from the plains of Bihar following industrialisation and consequential urbanisation of the area and successful operation of the then Congress Government to win over the leaders of the movement thwarted such attempt of the missionaries at least temporarily.

By mid sixties Hindu revivalists also took an initiative to establish their foothold in the region. They also opened schools and other socio-religious centres parallel to Christian institutions. Banking upon Sanskritisation model of anthropology, which was even supported by some foreign anthropologists that the tribes of the region have been the followers of Hinduism, the forces of Hindutva launched an aggressive campaign against the Christian missionaries. Foreign writers like Ghurey (1943) and others on the basis of data collected by Dalton (1872) and Risley (1891) built up a theory of tribal society and culture as merely an underdeveloped form of Hindu society and culture.

By mid eighties Jharkhand movement reached a low ebb and proselytisation programme of the Christian missionaries was substantially contained due to planned opposition of Hindu revivalists. Besides, the Hindu revivalists succeeded in re-conversion of sizeable number of tribals and as a result the Christian missionaries suffered from a sort of frustration and demoralisation. In 1986, however the visit of Pope to Ranchi and other parts of India was a moral booster for the Church functionaries.

Taking up the challenge of the forces of Hindutva as an alarm signal, the Christian missionaries made some tactical changes to counter their adversaries. They switched over from socio-religious activities to politico-religious mode and even joined hands with the forces of Left extremists. Christian missionaries always treated the Communists as untouchables.

However, when western lobby pampered the Left extremists for their anti Russian stand, Christian institutions also gave them shelter in Church sponsored voluntary organisations. The move was to fight against the growing influence of the Hindu revivalists among the tribals. Another tactical move of Christian Missions was tribalisation of Christianity in one hand and Sanskritisation of the names of their institutions on the other.

Giving Hindu names to the converts during Baptisation, allowing the women folk to imitate their Hindu counterparts in dress/ gestures, Sanskrit names to various Christian institutions like Nirmala College, Satya Bharati, Nirmal Hriday, Jan Vikas Mandal and Vikas Maitree and allowing the converts for participation in animistic celebration of non-Christian tribals were part of such tactical move of the missionaries.

Missionaries with the support of the Leftist forces, who subscribe to the modernisation theory of anthropology that the tribes of the region were indigenous settlers, created a situation, which led to confrontations between the tribal Christians and the Hindu-non-tribals. Such Christian-Hindu encounter accelerated the process for turning incendiary, which gradually widened the ethnic divide in the region.

Taking advantage of the situation, foreign funded organisations like Indian Social Institute, an outfit of Roman Catholic Mission, William Carries and others with lot of financial resources in their possession accelerated the process of tribalisation of Jharkhand politics. They organised seminars and workshops for propagating the alleged plight of the tribals and training camps for the target group of tribal youths for their infiltration in various Social Actions and Christian Actions Groups.

With a view to mobilise the tribal people against various development projects launched by the Government in the region, Christian missionaries highlighted the danger of further influx of non-tribal population with such projects. They created apprehension of displacement in tribal mind and abandonment of their 'Sarana and Sasan' (the places of worship). Tribal political leaders on the other hand were convinced that influx of non-tribal population would adversely affect the demography of the region, which consequently would affect the hegemony of tribal voters in the constituency. They accordingly organised seminars, symposia and workshops to oppose the various developmental projects like Koel Karo Hydel project, Kutku Dam project and Paras Dam project initiated in the region by the government. The move was to counter the attempt of the contemporary governments of post-colonial India to integrate the tribes in the mainstream developmental process of the country.

Competitive experiments of Westernisation and Indianisation of the tribals by the respective forces created confusion in tribal society and thereby prompted a new generation of tribal youths to adopt the path of extreme tribalism. They wanted tribal veto in each and every process of development in the region. Meanwhile a new concept of applied anthropology with a theory that tribals were indigenous people of the land with separate nationality gave a new issue of tribal nationalism to tribal youths. Any attempt on the part of the Government for scientific transformation of tribal society was viewed by the new generation as its ethnocentric bias against the growing urge of tribal nationalism.

This new concept being closer to modernisation model of anthropology and an ingredient of westernisation also supported the theory of the Leftists that India was not one nation but a combination of several separate nationalities. It therefore, suited the politico-religious design of the Christian missionaries in containing the process of re-conversion by the Hindu revivalists.

Tribals of Jharkhand are now passing through a serious transition both socially and politically. They are not found content even with creation of new state of Jharkhand. On one hand the advent of Christianity disintegrated their life style and on the other the concerted effort of Christian missionaries to maintain their cultural hegemony over them gradually changed their outlook. The Christian converts within the community interpreted their indigenous life style befitting to Christian tradition without taking into account the negative impact of proselytisation, westernisation and de-tribalisation of the community.

Christian-tribal leaders, who on account of their education were more vocal than others, dominated Jharkhand politics for a long time. However, in due course of time, when non-Christian leadership started showing results, it turned into political as well as civilisational conflict.

Accepting the Christian tradition, the community-centric tribal society became individual centric, which led to ethnic conflicts. Instead of strengthening the country with the concept of Indian nationalism, concept of tribal nationalism became the socio-political ideology of the people. Dr. Nirmal Minz, a noted tribal church leader in his write-up - "Passing Scene of Chhotanagpur" consciously avoided these negative impacts of Christianity on the homogenous life style of tribal society.

The politico-religious march of the Christian missionaries and their encounter with Hindu-revivalists pushed the people of Jharkhand to a position, which has enormous potentiality to widen the ethnic divide in the region.

Political parties with their eyes on votes are no more interested in social integration of tribals with non- tribals. Urge for tribalisation of Jharkhand, which is a reflection of accumulated hatred against non-tribals has deeply penetrated the tribal mind.

This can be judged from a tribal saying quoted by Dr. Ram Dayal Munda, former Vice-Chancellor of Ranchi University and a widely travelled tribal intellectual in his article "Tribal Change and Development' that " He (non-tribal) enters like a needle and gets out like ploughshare". The new breed of tribal intellectuals, with the support of Christian outfits attends various seminars and workshops organised by international forums and put forward their views against the alleged ethnocentric policy of the Government.

Instead of making a concerted effort to develop an institutional mechanism to thwart the attempt of divisive forces in the region, the political leadership in the state is helping them due to their vote bank politics, which is apparently a danger signal for peace and harmony in the state. This is the reality of the ongoing problem in Jharkhand State and the Centre needs to pay more attention to the current conflict.

JHARKHAND POLITICS

Jharkhand politics has been at the center of interest right from early days of the state's creation, following its breakaway form Bihar in 2000.

Politics in Jharkhand has an old history. It has been the site of many tribal revolutions right from the British days and it was a similar kind of insurgence that led to the creation of the independent state of Jharkhand.

However, modern day Jharkhand politics feature an electoral system, divided between the assembly and parliamentary constituencies of the state, where many political parties compete for power. In fact, Jharkhand politics feature a number of political parties virtually unmatched by any other state in India.

Jharkhand Constituencies

Jharkhand has 14 parliamentary constituencies and as many as 81 assembly constituencies, distributed over the 12 districts of the state. The winners from the parliamentary constituencies go on to represent the state in the lower house of India's bicameral legislative structure and the winners form the assembly constituencies and become member of the state legislative assembly. The 2005 assembly elections saw a wing by the BJP led NDA coalition, defeating the UPA coalition, led by the INC. The result was seen to be consistent with the results of the 2004 general elections in India. The results of the general elections in Jharkhand were not concurrent with the large scale anti-incumbency felt across India that brought the UPA to power. The success was accorded to a large degree of popularity of the JMM, the state party in the politics of Jharkhand.

Political Parties in Jharkhand

Jharkand elections see the participation of many national, state and registered political parties. Almost all national level parties take interest in Jharkhand politics. Indian National Congress (INC), Bharatiya Janata Party (BJP) and Communist Party of India (CPI) are some of the most prominent presence of national parties in Jharkhand politics. Jharkhand Mukti Morcha (JMM) is the largest of the state level political parties. Many of the regional parties, which are registered but with minimum political impact as of now, also take a keen interest in the politics at Jharkhand.

LIST OF CHIEF MINISTERS (CM) OF JHARKHAND

S.N.	CM of Jharkhand	From	To	Party
1	Babulal Marandi Ramgarh	Nov 15, 2000	Mar 17, 2003	BJP
2	Arjun Munda Kharsawan	Mar 18, 2003	Mar 2, 2005	BJP
3	Shibu Soren	Mar 2, 2005	Mar 12, 2005	JMM
4	Arjun Munda Kharsawan	Mar 12, 2005	Sep 14, 2006	BJP
5	Madhu Koda Jaganathpur	Sep 14, 2006	Aug 23, 2008	IND
6	Shibu Soren	Aug 27, 2008	Jan 18, 2009	JMM
	President's rule	Jan 19, 2009	Dec 29, 2009	
7	Shibu Soren	Dec 30, 2009	May 31, 2010	JMM
	President's rule	Jun 1, 2010	Sep 11, 2010	
8	Arjun Munda Kharsawan	Sep 11, 2010	Jan 18, 2013	BJP
	President's rule	Jan 18, 2013	Jul 12, 2013	
9	Hemant Soren Dumka	Jul 13, 2013	Dec 23, 2014	JMM
10	Raghubar Das	Dec 28, 2014	Present	BJP

LIST OF GOVERNORS OF JHARKHAND

This is a List of Governors of Jharkhand since its inception on 15 November 2000.

Governors of Jharkhand

#	Name	Took Office	Left Office
1	Prabhat Kumar	15 November 2000	3 February 2002(year is error kindly correct it)
2	V.C Pande (Additional Charge)	4 February 2002	14 July 2002
3	M. Rama Jois	15 July 2002	11 June 2003
4	Ved Marwah	12 June 2003	9 December 2004
5	Syed Sibtey Razi	10 December 2004	25 July 2009
6	Kateekal Sankaranarayanan	26 July 2009	21 January 2010
7	M.O. Hasan Farook Maricar	22 January 2010	3 September 2011
8	Syed Ahmed	4 September 2011	17 May 2015
9	Draupadi Murmu	18 May 2015	incumbent

4

Language and Literature

LANGUAGE

Main languages of Jharkand
Khortha (23.46%)
Hindi (21.42%)
Santali (9.91%)
Bengali (9.74%)
Nagpuri (7.23%)
Urdu (5.96%)
Magahi (4.14%)
Ho (3.01%)
Mundari (2.93%)
Kurukh (2.89%)
Bhojpuri (2.29%)
Odia (1.61%)
Panch Pargania (0.74%)
Others (4.67%)

Hindi is the official language in Jharkhand. Jharkhand has accorded second language status to Angika, Bengali, Bhojpuri, Ho, Kharia, Kurukh, Khortha, Kurmali, Magahi, Maithili, Mundari, Nagpuri, Odia, Santali and Urdu.

RACE, RELIGION AND LANGUAGE

The absence of neat classifications of Adivasis as a homogenous social-cultural category and the intensely fluid nature of non-Adivasis are evident in the insuperable difficulty in arriving at a clear anthropological definition of a tribal in India, be it in terms of ethnicity, race, language, social forms or modes of livelihood.

The major waves of ingress into India divide the tribal communities into Veddids, similar to the Australian aborigines, and the Paleamongoloid Austro-Asiatic from the north-east. The third were the Greco-Indians who spread across Gujarat, Rajasthan and Pakistan from Central Asia. The fourth is the Negrito group of the Andaman Islands - the Great Andamanese, the Onge, the Jarawa and the Sentinelese who flourished in these parts for some 20,000 years but who could well become extinct soon. The Great Andamanese have been wiped out as a viable community with about only 30 persons alive as are the Onges who are less than a 100.

In the mid-Indian region, the Gond who number over 5 million, are the descendants of the dark skinned Kolarian or Dravidian tribes and speak dialects of Austric language family as are the Santhal who number 4 million. The Negrito and Austroloid people belong to the Mundari family of Munda, Santhal, Ho, Ashur, Kharia, Paniya, Saora etc. The Dravidian groups include the Gond, Oraon, Khond, Malto, Bhil, Mina, Garasia, Pradhan etc. and speak Austric or Dravidian family of languages. The Gujjar and Bakarwal descend from the Greco Indians and are interrelated with the Gujjar of Gujarat and the tribes settled around Gujranwala in Pakistan.

There are some 200 indigenous peoples in the north-east. The Boro, Khasi, Jantia, Naga, Garo and Tripiri belong to the Mongoloid stock like the Naga, Mikir, Apatani, Boro, Khasi, Garo, Kuki, Karbi etc. and speak languages of the Tibeto-Burman language groups and the Mon Khmer.

The Adi, Aka, Apatani, Dafla, Gallong, Khamti, Monpa, Nocte, Sherdukpen, Singpho, Tangsa, Wancho etc. of Arunachal Pradesh and the Garo of Meghalaya are of Tibeto-Burman stock while the Khasi of Meghalaya belong to the Mon Khmer group. In the southern region, the Malayali, Irula, Paniya, Adiya, Sholaga, Kurumba etc. belong to the proto-Australoid racial stock speaking dialects of the Dravidian family.

The Census of India 1991 records 63 different denominations as "other" of over 5.7 million people of which most are Adivasi religions. Though the Constitution recognises them as a distinct cultural group, yet when it comes to religion those who do not identify as Christians, Muslims or Buddhists are compelled to register themselves as Hindus. Hindus and Christians have interacted with Adivasis to civilize them, which has been defined as sanscritisation and westernisation.

However, as reflected during the 1981 census it is significant that about 5% of the Adivasis registered their religion by the names of their respective tribes or the names adopted by them. In 1991 the corresponding figure rose to about 10% indicating the rising consciousness and assertion of identity!

Though Article 350A of the Constitution requires primary education to be imparted in mother tongue, in general this has not been imparted except in areas where the Adivasis have been assertive. NCERT, the state owned premier education research centre has not shown any interest. With the neglect of Adivasi languages, the State and the dominant social order aspire to culturally and socially emasculate the Adivasis subdued by the dominant cultures. The Anthropological Survey of India reported a loss of more than two-thirds of the spoken languages, most of them tribal.

Fragmentation Some of the ST peoples of Himachal Pradesh, Uttar Pradesh, W. Bengal, Sikkim, Arunachal Pradesh, Nagaland, Manipur and Mizoram have their counterparts across the border in China (including Tibet), Bhutan, Myanmar and Bangladesh. The political aspirations of these trans-border tribes who find themselves living in different countries as a result of artificial demarcation of boundaries by erstwhile colonial rulers continue to be ignored despite the spread and proliferation of militancy, especially in the north east, making it into a conflict zone.

The Adivasi territories have been divided amongst the states formed on the basis of primarily the languages of the mainstream caste society, ignoring the validity of applying the same principle of language for the Adivasis in the formation of states. Jharkhand has been divided amongst Bihar, West Bengal, Madhya Pradesh and Orissa though the Bihar part of Jharkhand has now become a separate state after decades of struggle. The Gond region has been divided amongst Orissa, Andhra, Maharashtra and Madhya Pradesh. Similarly the Bhil region has been divided amongst Maharashtra, Madhya Pradesh, Gujarat and Rajasthan.

In the north-east, for example, the Naga in addition are divided into Nagaland, Manipur, Assam and Arunachal Pradesh. Further administrative sub-divisions within the states into districts, talukas and panchayats have been organised in such a way that the tribal concentration is broken up which furthers their marginalisation both physically and politically.

The 1874 "Scheduled District Act", the 1919 "Government of India Act" and later the "Government of India Act" of 1935 classified the hill areas as excluded and partially excluded areas where the provincial legislature had no jurisdiction. These formed the basis for the Article 244 under which two separate schedules *viz.* the V Schedule and the VI Schedule were incorporated for provision of a certain degree of self-governance in designated tribal majority areas. However, in effect this remained a non-starter. However, the recent legislation of the Panchayat Raj (Extension to the Scheduled Areas) Act of 1996 has raised hope of a radical redefinition of self-governance.

By not applying the same yard stick and norms for Adivasis as for the upper caste dominated mainstream, by not genuinely recognizing the Adivasis' traditional self-governing systems and by not being serious about devolving autonomy, the Indian State and society indicates a racist and imperialist attitude.

The call for a socially homogenous country, particularly in the Hindi Hindu paradigm have suppressed tribal languages, defiled cultures and destroyed civilisations.

The creation of a unified albeit centralised polity and the extension of the formal system of governance have emasculated the self-governing institutions of the Adivasis and with it their internal cohesiveness.

The struggle for the future, the conceptual vocabulary used to understand the place of Adivasis in the modern world has been constructed on the feudal, colonial and imperialistic notions which combines traditional and historical constructs with the modern construct based on notions of linear scientific and technological progress.

Historically the Adivasis, as explained earlier, are at best perceived as sub-humans to be kept in isolation, or as 'primitives' living in remote and backward regions who should be "civilized". None of them have a rational basis. Consequently, the official and popular perception of Adivasis is merely that of isolation in forest, tribal dialect, animism, primitive occupation, carnivorous diet, naked or semi-naked, nomadic habits, love, drink and dance.

Contrast this with the self-perception of Adivasis as casteless, classless and egalitarian in nature, community-based economic systems, symbiotic with nature, democratic according to the demands of the times, accommodative history and people-oriented art and literature.

The significance of their sustainable subsistence economy in the midst of a profit oriented economy is not recognised in the political discourse, and the negative stereotyping of the sustainable subsistence economy of Adivasi societies is based on the wrong premise that the production of surplus is more progressive than the process of social reproduction in co-existence with nature.

The source of the conflicts arises from these unresolved contradictions. With globalisation, the hitherto expropriation of rights as an outcome of development has developed into expropriation of rights as a precondition for development. In response, the struggles for the rights of the Adivasis have moved towards the struggles for power and a redefinition of the contours of state, governance and progress.

SADRI LANGUAGE

Sadri (also Nagpuri) is an Eastern Indo-Aryan language spoken by the Sadan in the Indian states of Jharkhand, Bihar, Chhattisgarhand Odisha.

In addition to native speaker, Sadri is also used as a lingua-fraca by large number of tribal groups such as: Kharia, Munda, Bhumij, Kurukh and many of these tribal group have adopted Sadri as their first language. It spoken by many Tea-tribes of Assam, West Bengal and Bangladesh.

Etymology

The origin of Sadan/Sadri and other related terms is somewhat obscure. Probably the term "Sadan" derive from nisaada, referring to an ethnic group of Northeast India. The name Nagpur is probably taken from Nagvanshi, who ruled in this part of the country.

Geographical Distribution

Nagpuri language is chiefly spoken in western Chota Nagpur Plateau region of west-central Jharkhand in districts such as Latehar, Lohardaga, Chatra, Palamu, Garhwa, Gumla,Simdega, Ranchi, Khunti, West Singhbhum, North-east Chhattisgarh in district Jashpur, Surguja, Balrampur, South-east Uttarpradesh in Sonbhadra, Northern Odisha in Sundargarhand south-west Bihar in Aurangabad district.

History

Nagpuri language evolved from Prakrit languages. During reign of Nagvanshi kings, It was language of royal court.

Script

Nagpuri is commonly written in the Devanagari script, an abugida. Devanagari consists of 11 vowels and 33 consonants and written from left to right.

Vocabulary

The main source Nagpuri lexicon is Prakrit and Sanskrit. During the medieval period contact with North India resulted in introduction of some Persian words.

LANGUAGE OF JHARKHAND

Almost all the major languages of Jharkhand possess a connecting link with the Indo-Aryan languages. As a matter of fact, the language of Jharkhand has descended from three major families of dialects. The prime lingos which predominate in Jharkhand include Oriya, Urdu, Nagpuri, Bengali, Bhojpuri, Khortha, Sadri and Angika. These languages in Jharkhand are also very easy to master and convenient to speak with absolute fluency.

Angika is considered to be a language that bears significant resemblance with the 'Cham', a dialect chiefly spoken in Cambodia, Malaysia, Thailand, Vietnam and many more places. Actually it has been categorized into Bihari languages.

This language of Jharkhand known as Bhojpuri has a lot of similitude with the lingos like Urdu, Hindi and Sanskrit. International venues like Guyana, Tobago, Surinam, Mauritius and Fuji have adopted Bhojpuri as one of their principle dialects.

The rest of the Indo-Aryan languages like Bengali, Sadri, Oriya and Hindi are also closely linked.

Amongst other common languages at Jharkhand, the Munda languages also have quite a few speakers as well. This particular bunch of languages belongs to the Austro-Asiatic family of languages. The chief feature of the Mundari language that precisely demarcates it from the rest of the dialects includes the use of a trio of grammatical numbers and two animate and inanimate genders. Other languages that belong to this group include Mundari, Ho and Santali.

The Dravidian group of languages approximately includes 73 different lingoes, amongst which Oraon, Paharia and Korwa have penetrated into the household of quite a few residents of Jharkhand.

Santhali

The dialect regarded as Santhali is chiefly and most fluently spoken by the Austro-Asiatic individuals inhabiting the domain of Jharkhand, who possess a blood-line of the Munda sub-family. But the lingo regarded as Santhali is also spoken by the residents of other states like Assam, Tripura, West Bengal, Orissa and Bihar.

This language called Santhali in Jharkhandbears a strong resemblance with the rest of the languages spoken in Jharkhand which includes Mundari, Khorta and many more. As a matter of fact, it has been estimated that approximately, six million individuals, dispersed across some of the major countries like Nepal, Bhutan, India and Bangladesh take a lot of pride in speaking this language of Santhali of Jharkhand.

Bengali

Bengali or Bangla is one of the most important languages in the entire state of Jharkhand in India. The language of Bengali in Jharkhand belongs to the Indic group of languages. The Indic group of languages is again a part of the Aryan or the Indo-Iranian group of languages.

The Aryan or the Indo-Iranian group of languages belongs to the family of languages called the Indo-European language family. The language of Bengali is a modified version of the

Apabhramsa-Avahatta. The language of Apabhramsa-Avahatta has been one of the most important languages in the eastern part of the subcontinent of India.

The use of punctuation in the language of Bengali of Jharkhand is identical to that of the English language. The only exception is the usage of the punctuation mark of full stop. The full stop is replaced by a 'dari' in the language of Jharkhand Bengali.

The language of Bengali at Jharkhand offers a number of constructions of sentences that are impersonalized. The language of Bengali does not have different expressions for 'the' and 'a'. This characteristic of the language of Bengali in Jharkhand makes it similar to the Slavonic languages.

Karmali

Karmali is one of the languages spoken in the state of Jharkhand in India. The language of Karmali is also called Khole. This dialect is actually a classification of the Santali language, which is one of the most important tribal languages in the subcontinent of India. The Santali language is again a type of Munda language. The language of Munda belongs to the family of languages called the Austro-Asiatic language family.

There are some languages that have close associations with the Karmali of Jharkhand. Some of these languages are Lohari-Santali, Kamari-Santali, Paharia, Manjhi and Mahali or Mahli. All these languages fall under the category of Santali language.

The people of Jharkhand who speak the language of Karmali in Jharkhand basically belong to one of the scheduled tribes of India. The people who speak Karmali at Jharkhand have two main ways of living. These are daily labor and cultivation. The Karmali speaking people of Jharkhand have faith in two major religions. These are Christianity and Hinduism. Hinduism is the chief religion for these people and there are some people who have faith in Christianity.

Khariya

Khariya is one of the many tribal languages spoken by the ethnic inhabitants of Jharkhand. The Khariya group of people in Jharkhand is located in and around the Chota Nagpur valley regions and forms a major linguistic and ethnic group in the state. Khariya in Jharkhand is also spoken in parts of Orissa and belongs to the Austro-Asiatic group of languages.

Despite the colonial influences operative in the state, Khariya in Jharkhand has remained practically unchanged over the years. The three sub-groups in which the Khariyas are divided include the Dudh Kheriya, the Dhelki Kheirya and the Hill Kheriya. In the recent years, social activists and researches have brought Khariya back into the limelight. East Singbhum, Gumla, Simdega and Hazaribagh are districts of Jharkhand that are the areas where most of the speakers of Khariya of Jharkhand are located. Khariya customs are intrinsically related to the language and the Khariya of Jharkhand is usually employed in carrying out the major rites of the region. The speakers of Khariya at Jharkhand are also fairly proficient in the use of languages like Hindi and Bengali, according to the areas of their inhabitation.

Mundari

Regarded as one of the chief languages of Jharkhand, Mundari also serves to be the mother tongue of the individuals who hail from the Munda tribe who primarily inhabit the eastern and central realms of India. As a matter of fact, Mundari shares a lot of features with another very common language known as Santhali.

Mundari of Jharkhand along with Santhali are considered to be two of those languages that have originated from Austro-Asiatic languages. Mundari in Jharkhand is most frequently spoken by the Munda people who are topologically confined to the domain of Jharkhand. However, it has also dispersed across the Indian turf and conquered territories in Orissa, West Bengal,

Chattisgarh and Bihar. Some of them have also shifted their permanent abode to Bangladesh as well.

The dialect known as Mundari at Jharkhand bears tremendous resemblance with other languages like Sanskrit and Dravidian. The language Mundari at Jharkhand has also been affected by a bifurcation that had caused it to get separated into North and South Munda with the former spoken primarily in the region that is marked by Chota Nagpur Plateau that spans across the state of West Bengal, Orissa and Jharkhand and the latter spoken in the central fringe of Orissa.

5

Geography and Flora & Fauna

GEOGRAPHY

Geography of Jharkhand is comprised of the rich mineral resources and the highly agricultural prospect in this state.

A River in Jharkhand

Geography of Jharkhand is comprises of the Chota Nagpur Plateau, which is the source of the Koel River, Damodar River, Brahmani River, Kharkai River, and Subarnarekha rivers, whose upper watersheds lie within Jharkhand. Much of the state is still covered by forest. Forest preserves support populations of Royal Bengal Tiger and Asian Elephant. Soil content of Jharkhand state mainly consist of soil formed from disintegration of rocks and stones, and soil composition is further divided into:

1. Red soil, found mostly in the Damodar Valley, and Rajmahal Hillarea 2. Micacious soil (containing particles of mica), found in Koderma District, Jhumeritilaiya Barkagaon, and areas around the Mandar hill. 3. Sandy soil, generally found in Hazaribagh and Dhanbad 4. Black soil, found in Rajmahal area. 5. Laterite soil, found in western part of Ranchi, Palamu District, and parts of Santhal Parganas and Singhbhum District.

Palash flowers, bright red, pepper the skyline in Jharkhand during fall, also known as forest fire

Jharkhand is located in the eastern part of India and is enclosed by Bihar to the northern side, Chhattisgarh and Uttar Pradesh to the western side, Odisha to the southern part and West Bengal to the eastern part.

Jharkhand envelops a geographical area of 79.70 lakh hectare. Much of Jharkhand lies on the Chota Nagpur Plateau. Many rivers pass through the Chota Nagpur plateau. They are: Damodar, North Koel, South Koel, Sankh, Brahmani and Subarnarekha rivers. The higher watersheds of these rivers stretch out within the Jharkhand state. Much of the Jharkhand state is still enclosed by forest. Forests sustain the population of Elephants and tigers.

A Female Indian Elephant at Dalma Wildlife Sanctuary in Jharkhand

The new state of Jharkhand largely comprises of the forest tracks of Chhotanagpur plateau and Santhal Pargana and has distinct cultural traditions. This area in and around the districts of Chhotanagpur and Santhal Parganas was formerly Southern Bihar and is thickly wooded and consists of a succession of hills. Out of the area of 79.7 lakh hectares, the cultivable land is 38 lakh hectares and the present net sown area is 18.04 lakh hectares.

The net irrigated area is only 1.57 lakh hectares which is 8 per cent of the net sown area. More than 29 per cent land is covered by forest area. Although Jharkhand is endowed with vast and rich natural resources, mainly minerals and forest, 80 per cent of its population residing in 32620 villages depend mainly on agriculture and allied activities for their livelihood. Horticulture is one of the important sub-sectors of agriculture, having ample scope for expansion in Jharkhand.

The total area occupied by various plantation and horticulture (P&H) crop in the State is about 2.57 lakh hectares with an estimated total production of 37.85 lakh tonnes. Different kinds of fruit crops are grown in Jharkhand. The State has a forage seed production farm at Chatra. There is also a feed plant in Ranchi which manufactures and supplies adult cattle feed (ACF) and bypass protein feed (BPF) to the farmers on cost basis.

Most of the state lies on the Chota Nagpur Plateau, which is the source of the Koel, Damodar, Brahmani, Kharkai, and Subarnarekha rivers, whose upper watersheds lie within Jharkhand. Much of the state is still covered by forest. Forest preserves support populations of tigers and Asian Elephants.

Soil content of Jharkhand state mainly consist of soil formed from disintegration of rocks and stones, and soil composition is further divided into:

1. Red soil, found mostly in the Damodar valley, and Rajmahal area
2. Micacious soil (containing particles of mica), found in Koderma, Jhumeritilaiya, Barkagaon, and areas around the Mandar hill
3. Sandy soil, generally found in Hazaribagh and Dhanbad
4. Black soil, found in Rajmahal area
5. Laterite soil, found in western part of Ranchi, Palamu, and parts of Santhal Parganas and Singhbhum

CLIMATE

Climate of Jharkhand varies from Humid subtropical in the north to tropical wet and dry in the south-east. The main seasons are summer, rainy, autumn, winter and spring. The summer lasts from mid-April to mid-June. May, the hottest month, characterized by daily high temperatures around 38 °C(100° F) and low temperatures around 25° C (77° F). The southwest monsoon, from mid-June to October, brings nearly all the state's annual rainfall, which ranges from about 40 inches (1,000 mm) in the west-central part of the state to more than 60 inches (1,500 mm) in the southwest. Rainfall on the plateau is generally heavier than on the plains. Nearly half of the annual precipitation falls in July and August.The winter season lasts from November to February with average minimum temperatures around 10 °C (50 °F). The temperatures in Ranchi in December usually vary from about 10 °C (50 °F) to around 24° C (75° F). Spring season lasts from mid-february to mid-April.

Hills and Mountain Ranges

- Parasnath: Parasnath Hill is also recognized as Sri Sammed Sikharji. The Parasnath Hill is situated in Giridih district of Jharkhand. It is a chief Jain pilgrimage site and the holy place for Jains. It is believed in the Jain culture that 20 of the 24 Tirthankaras attained Moksha from this place. The height of the hill is 1,350 meters.
- Netarhat: Netarhat is a town in Latehar district. Referred to as the "Queen of Chotanagpur", It is a popular hill station.It is famous for its glorious sunrises and sunsets.
- Trikut: Trikut Hill is located ten kilometers away from Deoghar and lies on the way to Dumka in Jharkhand. Trikut hill is also called Trikutchal because there are 3 major peaks on the hill. The height of Trikut hill is 2470 feet.
- Ranchi Hill: The Ranchi Hill is an attractions in Ranchi, Jharkhand. At Ranchi Hill's pinnacle, there is a holy place dedicated to Lord Shiva. At the pedestal of the hill of Ranchi there is a lake, Ranchi Lake.
- Tagore Hill: The Tagore Hill is also recognized as the Morabadi Hill. The Tagore hill is located in Morabadi, Ranchi. The brother of Rabindranath Tagore, Jyotirindranath Tagore had made a tour at Ranchi in the year 1908.
- Canary Hill: Canary Hill is surrounded by parks and has 3 tiny lakes. Canary hill has a surveillance tower. From the hill's top there are views of the township.
- Nandan Hill: Nandan hill is a small hill binding the township which has a Nandi Temple. The Nandan hill is located in front of the Shiv temple. It is also surrounded by a lake.

- Fuldungri: Fuldungri is situated on a small hill near Ghatshila town. Fuldungri's peak has view of the nearby hills and valleys. Burudih Lake is situated seventeen kilometers North of Fuldungri.

Main Rivers

Dassam Falls near Ranchi is a tributary of Subarnarekha River.

- Son River: Origin of Son River: Amarkantak, Cities on the Shore of Sone River: Sidhi, Dehri, Patna
- Subarnarekha River: Origin of Subarnarekha River: Chota Nagpur Plateau, Cities on the Shore of Subarnarekha River: Chandil, Jamshedpur, Ghatshila, Gopiballavpur
- Damodar River: Origin of Damodar River: Chota Nagpur Plateau, Cities on the Shore of Damodar River: Bokaro, Asansol, Raniganj, Durgapur, Bardhaman
- North Koel River: Origin of North Koel River: Chota Nagpur plateau, Cities on Shore of North Koel River: Daltonganj
- South Koel River: Origin of South Koyal River: Chota Nagpur Plateau, Cities on the Shore of South Koyal River: Manoharpur, Rourkela
- Lilajan River : Also known as Falgu river. Origin of Lilajan River: Northern Chota Nagpur Plateau, City on the Shore: Gaya
- Ajay River: Origin of Ajay River: Munger, Cities on the Shore of Ajay River: Purulia, Chittaranjan, Ilambazar, Jaydev Kenduli

- Mayurakshi River: Origin of Mayurakshi River: Trikut hill, City on the Shore of Mayurakshi River: Suri

FLORA AND FAUNA

A crocodile at Muta crocodile breeding centre at Ormanjhi, Ranchi

Jharkhand has a rich variety of flora and fauna. The National Parks and the Zoological Gardens located in the state of Jharkhand present a panorama of this variety.

Part of the reason for the variety and diversity of flora and fauna found in Jharkhand state may be accredited to the Palamau Tiger Reservesunder the Project Tiger. This reserve is abode to hundreds of species of flora and fauna, as indicated within brackets: mammals (39), snakes (8), lizards (4), fish (6), insects (21), birds (170), seed bearing plants and trees (97), shrubs and herbs (46), climbers, parasites and semi-parasites (25), and grasses and bamboos (17).

Weather remains cool in most areas of Jharkhand, especially Ranchi, Gumla, Netarhat, Dhanbad etc. Jharkhand has a rich variety of Flora and Fauna. The National Parks and the Zoological Gardens located in the state of Jharkhand present a panorama of this variety.

Betla National Park (Palamu), 25 km from Daltonganj covers an area of about 250 square kilometres. The national park has a large variety of wild life like Tigers, Elephants, Bison locally called gaurs, Sambhar, hundreds of Wild boar and 15 to 20 feet long Python, herds of spotted Deer, Rabbits and Fox.

Part of the reason for the variety and diversity of flora and fauna found in Jharkhand state may be accredited to the Project Tiger Reserve of Palamu, which is abode to hundreds of species of flora and fauna. The Hazaribagh Wildlife Sanctuary or the Hazaribagh National Park, with scenic beauties, 135 km from Ranchi, is set in an ecosystem very similar to Betla National Park of Palamu.

Part of the reason for the variety and diversity of flora and fauna found in Jharkhand state may be accredited to the Project Tiger Reserve of Palamu, which is abode to hundreds of species of flora and fauna, as indicated within brackets: mammal, Snakes, Lizards, Fish, Insects, Birds, seed bearing Plants and Tress, Shrubs and Herbs, Climbers, Parasites and semi-Parasites and Grasses and Bamboo.

The Hazaribagh Wildlife Sanctuary, with scenic beauties, 135 km from Ranchi, is set in an ecosystem very similar to Betla National Park of Palamu.

One Zoological Garden is also located about 16 km from Ranchi, and a number of mammalian fauna have been collected there for visitors.

Jharkhand Flora and Fauna

Jharkhand flora and fauna have a rich variety. The territory of Jharkhand provides a panoramic view of a wide variety of flora and fauna housed within the territory. In fact, the national parks and the wildlife sanctuaries in Jharkhand offer a rich variety in terms of biodiversity.

Jharkhand Fauna

Jharkhand, which literally means 'the territory of forests', is known for its dense evergreen forests and wildlife. In fact, the state of Jharkhand is known to possess the richest evergreen forests in India. Statistics prove that about 200 species of avifauna is found in the territory of Jharkhand.

Fauna of Jharkhand

Among the major animals that form an integral part of Jharkhand flora and fauna are:

- Elephant
- Bison
- Wolf
- Antelope
- Rabbit
- Fox
- Sambhar
- Wild boar
- Python
- Squirrel
- Blue bull
- Mongoose
- Jackal
- Honey badger
- Malabar giant
- Tiger
- Deer
- Langur
- Rhesus
- Python
- Porcupine
- Wild cat, etc.

These animals are found in the national parks and wildlife sanctuaries of the territory. Some of the important animal reserves in Jharkhand are:

- Hazaribagh Wildlife Sanctuary
- Betla National Park, etc.

Jharkhand Flora

Moreover, talking about the flora of Jharkhand, it can be said that the Jharkhand flora mostly consists of dry and moist deciduous forests. It is noteworthy in this context that Jharkhand possess a semi-arid landscape, which suffers an acute shortage of water during the hot summer months: therefore, dry deciduous trees are common in the territory of Jharkhand. Among the important trees that form an important part of the fauna at Jharkhand are sal, jackfruit, jamun, kendu, gambhar, shisham, mahua, katha, lac, pesar, mango, aasan, baheda and bamboo.

Therefore, it is evident that the Jharkhand has rich store of flora and fauna that largely contributes towards the tourism within the state.

AJAY RIVER

Ajay River is a major river in Jharkhand and West Bengal. The word "Ajay" means "not conqurered"

Geography: It originates on a small hill about 300 metres high, south west of Munger in Bihar. It then flows through Jharkhand and enters West Bengal at Simjuri, near Chittaranjan. It first forms the border between Bardhaman District and Jharkhand and then between Bardhaman District and Birbhum District, and finally it enters Katwa subdivision of Bardhaman district at Nareng village in Ketugram police station. It then joins the Bhagirathi River. Total length of the Ajay is 288 km, out of which 152 km is in West Bengal.

The important tributaries of the Ajay are Pathro and Jayanti in Jharkhand, and Tumuni and Kunur in Bardhaman district of West Bengal.

The upper reaches of the Ajay pass through hilly regions with latte rite soil. It is only from Ausgram in Bardhaman district that the Ajay flows through alluvial plains. The Ajay valley was densely forested with sal, piyasal and palas trees till recent times when mining and other activities led to the clearing of forests.

History: In the history of ancient India edited by Mc Krindle, there was a river called Amystis that flows past a town called Katadupa, in the days of Megasthenes. Another historian Wilfred opines that Amystis is modern day Ajay. In recent times there has been exploration of the remains of an ancient civilisation similar to that of the Indus Valley Civilisation at Pandu Rajar Dhibi in the lower Ajay valley.

There has been at least 14 recorded floods in the 20th century in the Ajay river. The lower reaches of the river have embankments to prevent flooding.

Kendubillo, claimed to be the birth place of the 13th century Sanskrit poet Jayadeva of Geeta Govinda fame, and Churulia, birth place of Kazi Nazrul Islam are located on the banks of the Ajay.

BAITARANI RIVER

The Baitarani is one of six major rivers of Orissa, which lends its coastal plain the name of "Hexadeltaic region" or the "Gift of Six Rivers. These deltas divide the coastal plain into three regions from north to south. The Baitarani, along with the Mahanadi and the Brahmani forms the Middle Coastal Plain, which bears evidences of past 'back bays' and present lakes.

It originates from Guptaganga hills in Gonasika of Keonjhar district in Orissa state of India at an elevation of 900m above MSL. The upper most part of the river of about 80 km length flow in northerly direction then it changes its path suddenly by 900 and flow east ward. The beginning portion of Baitarani acts as the boundary between Orissa and Jharakhand.

The river enters plain at Anandpur and creates a deltaic zone at Akhuapada. The river travels a distance of 360 km to drain to the Bay of Bengal after joining of the Brahmani at Dhamra mouth near Chandabali. The river has in total 65 numbers of tributaries out of which 35 nos. join in left side and rest join in the right side. The river basin in Orissa is spread in 42 blocks of eight districts.

Major portion of its basin lies within the state of Orissa and small patch of the upper reach lies in the Jharkhand state. The upper Baitarani basin in western slopes of the Eastern Ghats consisting of the Panposh-Keonjhar-Pallahara plateau is one of the two plateaus forming 'The Central Plateaus'—one of Orissa's five major morphological regions.

Dams and barrages on the Baitarani and its major tributary, the Salandi irrigate 61,920 ha. The proposed Bhimkund and upper Baitarani multi-purpose projects envisage many more dams across this river and its tributaries to provide irrigation to more than 100,000 ha.

Flood is a regular phenomenon in the Baitarani basin and its inhabitants live with constant fears of loss to life and property. Even a two-day rain in July in 2005 made it overflowed its banks affecting 140,000 people in 220 villages of Jajpur and Bhadrak districts. There are also at least two other cases embankment breaching and marooning during this year inflicting massive loss to life and property. Apart from the long pending construction of dam at Bhimkund and proposed other measures like river bed excavation and construction of embankments etc. in the deltaic region, there remain an unaddressed needs of land use issues in the upstream, on which, till date, no serious thoughts or efforts have not been directed.

Baitarani basin with its rich mineral and agricultural sources and with availability of cheap labour, offered ideal ground for establishment and operation of various industrial units, however consequent principal activities in industrial, agricultural and mining sectors contributed significantly towards deterioration in the water quality.

BARAKAR RIVER

Bararkar River is the main tributary of Damodar River in eastern India. Originating near Padma in Hazaribagh district of Jharkhand it flows for 225 km across the northern part of the

Chota Nagpur plateau, mostly in a west to east direction, before joining the Damodar near Dishergarh in Bardhaman district of West Bengal. It has a catchment area of 6159 sq km. The main tributaries, Barsoti and Usri, flow in from the south and north respectively. Apart from the two main tributaries some fifteen medium/small streams join it.

The Barakar skirts the northern portion of Parashanth Hill, (1350 meters/4470 feet), the highest hill in the region, located in Giridih district of Jharkhand and a centre of Jain pilgrimage.

Fury of the River: The river flows in all fury during the rains in its upper reaches and has washed away two bridges constructed successively on the Grand Trunk Road. The great stone bridge across the river near Barhi, in Hazaribagh district, built around 1848, was washed away in 1913, after a fall of 10 inches of rain in 24 hours. The narrow iron bridge, which was built to replace it, withstood the strains of troop movement during the Second World War, but gave way in 1946, with another great flood. A new bridge built in the fifties has withstood the fury of the river.

There is another bridge on the Grand Trunk Road, across the Barakar, connecting Barakar, a small town bearing the same name in Bardhaman district of West Bengal with Chirkunda in Jharkhand. With heavy traffic in the heart of the coal belt, the bridge built in the mid 19th century is in need of repairs. A new bridge has been built, to the north, on the bypass running from Kalipahari, before entering Asansol to Nirsa in Dhanbad district.

The huge volume of monsoon water was carried down the valley and used to create havoc with floods in the lower Damodar basin. Annual rainfall over the basin varies between 765 and 1607 mm with an average of 1200 mm of which 80% occurs during the monsoon season from June to September. In order to harness the river (along with the Damodar), the Damodar Valley Corporation planned and implemented independent India's first multipurpose river valley project. The first dam of the project was constructed across the Barakar at Tilayia.

Dams and Power Stations

Tilayia: DVC's first dam was across the Barakar at Tilayia, in Hazaribagh district of Bihar, now in Jharkhand. It was inaugurated on 21 February 1953. The dam is 366 meters long and is 30.18 meters high from the river bed level. Tilaiya hydel power station is located on the left bank of the river Barakar. The structure is entirely of reinforced concrete. It has two generating units of 2 MW each with a provision for a third future unit of the same capacity.

Maithon: DVC's second dam was across the Konar River, a tributary of the Damodar, in Hazaribagh district, and the third was across the Barakar at Maithon in Dhanbad district of Bihar, now Jharkhand. The river forms the boundary between West Bengal and Jharkhand in that area. The dam was inaugurated on 27 September 1957. The dam (both concrete and earthen) is 4860 meters long and the concrete dam is 43.89 meters high above the river bed level. The unique feature of Maithon is that the hydel power station is located underground in the left bank of the river (on the West Bengal side) and is the first of its kind in India. The Power Station has a total generating capacity of 60 MW with three units of 20 MW each. About 13 km downstream from Maithon, the Barakar joins the Damodar.

Maithon Dam is 48 km from Dhanbad and around 25 km from Asansol. Other towns such as Salanpur, Chittaranjan and Kulti lie still nearer. It receives a steady and daily stream of tourists.

In order to augment the meagre hydroelectric power generation DVC has gone in for both gas turbine and thermal power generation. While most of its facilities for such generation lie in the Damodar region, Maithon in the Barakar regions is a major focal point. Maithon Gas Turbine Station was commissioned at Maithon in 1989. The station has an installed capacity of 82.5 MW with three units each of 27.5 MW capacity.

The 2 X 500 MW Maithon Right Bank thermal power

station is under implementation. It is a joint venture of Tata Power and DVC. A 2 X 500 MW greenfield thermal power station has been proposed for Koderma.

Proposed Dam at Balpahari: DVC is working on the proposal for a third dam across the Barakar at Balpahari in Jharkhand. Planned as part of its network of dams and barrages in the valley region, the Balpahari project was conceived with the objective of reducing siltation problems at Maithon, increasing the reach of canal irrigation and adding to hydro-electric generation capacity by 20 MW from the existing 144 MW.

Soil Conservation: After the construction of the four dams at Tilayia, Konar, Maithon and Panchet by DVC, it was observed that the rate of silt inflow into the reservoirs were much higher than what was anticipated earlier. It threatened the longevity of the reservoirs.

The catchment area of these reservoirs spread over the undulating terrain of the Chhotanagpur plateau is seriously affected by soil erosion. Large volume of silt in the form of coarse and fine sediment is removed from the area by erosion under the impact of the water flow caused by torrential rain, which runs down the numerous stream channels during the monsoon.

Thus the problem of reservoir siltation assumed great importance in the case of DVC. In order to prolong the life of the reservoirs, there was need for soil conservation and silt control. DVC set up a Soil Conservation Department at Hazaribagh to tackle the twin problems of reservoir siltation and soil deterioration in 1949.

Fisheries: The reservoirs at Tilaiya and Maithon, provided scope for development of fisheries. Efforts were made to introduce carps once the water accumulated behind the dams but the results have not been commensurate with the efforts, largely due to the formidable presence of predatory catfish W. attu and other predators such as Notopterus chitala and Barilius bola at Tilaiya, and catfishes Wallago attu and Aorichthys aor, at Maithon. These predators take a heavy toll of the stocked carps Trash and uneconomic fishes form dense population at Tilaiya reservoir, competing with major carps for food. Composition of catch at both the places is: catla, mrigala, rohita and calbasu.

CHHOTANAGPUR

Chhotanagpur is an area including the tribal areas of Jharkhand, Madhya Pradesh, Orissa, and West Bengal states in India. Many residents of the area identify with the name even though there is no political recognition of the area. A local dialect of Hindi called Nagpuri is common in the area.

Chhotanagpur Plateau: The Chhotanagpur Plateau (also Chhota Nagpur) is a plateau in eastern India, which covers much of Jharkhand state as well as adjacent parts of Orissa, Bihar, and Chhattisgarh. The Indo-Gangetic plain lies to the north and east of the plateau, and the basin of the Mahanadi River lies to the south. There are beautiful waterfalls such as Lodh Falls. The plateau is made up of ancient Precambrian rocks. Deposits of Coal support the industries of the Damodar Valley. Chota Nagpur is made up of three smaller plateaus, the Ranchi, Hazaribagh, and Kodarma plateaus. The Ranchi plateau is the largest of the plateaus, with an average elevation of 700 meters. The total area of Chota Nagpur is approximately 65,000 sq km.

Much of the plateau is forested, with Sal trees predominant, and is covered by the Chota Nagpur dry deciduous forest ecoregion. The plateau is one of the few remaining refuges left in India for tigers and Asian Elephants.

DAMODAR RIVER

Damodar River originates near Chandwa village, Palamau district, on the Chota Nagpur Plateau in the Jharkhand state in eastern India and flows eastward for about 592 km through the states of Jharkhand and West Bengal to the estaury of the River Hughli. It has a number of tributaries and subtributaries, such as Barakar, Konar, Guaia, Jamania, Usri, Bokaro, Haharo, Khadia and Bhera.

In some of the local languages of Jharkhand it is called Damuda, damu means sacred and da means water. The Damodar earlier used to flow through Bengal on a direct west to east course and join the River Hughli near Kalna. However, it has changed its course and in its lower reaches most of the water flows into the Mundeswari river, which combines with other rivers and finally most of the Damodar water flows into the Rupnarayan River. The balance water flows through what is known as Damodar into the Hughli south of Kolkata.

The Barakar is the most important tributary of the Damodar. It originates near Padma in Hazaribagh district and flows through Jharkhand before meeting the Damodar near Dishergarh in West Bengal. The Damodar and the Barakar trifurcates the Chota Nagpur plateau. The rivers pass through hilly areas with great force, sweeping away whatever lies in their path. Two bridges on the Grand Trunk Road near Barhi in Hazaribagh district were torn down by the Barakar, the great stone bridge in 1913 and the subsequent iron bridge in 1946.

Sorrow of Bengal: The Chota Nagpur Plateau recrives an average annual rainfall of around 1400 mm, almost all of it in the monsoon months between June and August. The huge volume of water that flows down the Damodar and its tributaries during the monsoons used to be a fury in the upper reaches of the valley but in the lower valley it used to overflow its banks and flood large areas.

Damodar River was earlier known as the Sorrow of Bengal as it used to flood many areas of Bardhaman, Hughli, Howrah and Medinipur districts. Even now the floods sometimes affect the lower Damodar Valley but the havoc it wreaked in earlier years is now a matter of history.

The floods were virtually an annual ritual but in some years the damage was probably more and so many of the great floods of the Damodar are recorded in history - 1770, 1855, 1866, 1873-74, 1875-76, 1884-85, 1891-92, 1897, 1900, 1907, 1913, 1927, 1930, 1935 and 1943. In four of these floods (1770, 1855, 1913 and 1943) most of Bardhaman town was flodded.

In 1789 an agreement was signed between Maharaja Kirti Chand of Burdwan and the East India Company wherein the Maharaja was asked to pay an additional amount of Rs. 1,93,721 for the construction and maintenance of embankment to prevent floods.

However, these ran into dispute and in 1866 and 1873, The Bengal Embankment Act was passed, transferring the powers to build and maintain embankemnt to the government.

So great was the deavstation every year that the floods passed into folklore, as the following Bhadu (popular folklore in the region) song testifies:

asara maasey chaas koirechhi
anbo bhadu bhadore.
damudare baan dekkechhe
kheya lau nai chole.
hei damudar pae pori
tuchka tumi baan kamao.
bachhor pore bhadu asbek
lau bukey bhaste dao.
We have sown the crops in Asar
We will bring Bhadu in Bhadra.
Floods have swollen the Damodar
The sailing boats cannot sail.
O Damodar! We fall at your feet
Reduce the floods a little.
Bhadu will come a year later
Let the boats sail on your surface.

Damodar Valley: The Damodar Valley is spread across Hazaribagh, Koderma, Giridih, Dhanbad, Bokaro and Chatra districts in Jharkhand and Bardhaman and Hooghly districts in

West Bengal and partially covers Palamu, Ranchi, Lohardaga and Dumka districts in Jharkhand and Howrah, Bankura and Purulia districts in West Bengal with a command area of 24,235 sq km.

The Damodar Valley contains large reserves of coal and mica, and the area is a highly developed industrial belt. Many refer to the Damodar Valley as the Ruhr of India because of its similarities with the Ruhr mining-industrial area of Germany. The dams on the Damodar River have several hydrelectric power plants. Of late, the Damodar has become one of the most polluted rivers of India, with chemicals, mine rejects and toxic effluents flowing into the river from mines and industries located in the valley. Efforts are being made to reduce the level of pollution in the river

The Damodar Valley lies in the Chota Nagpur Plateau of the state of Jharkhand, India. It also extends to some parts of the state of West Bengal. The valley derives its name from the Damodar River, which arises from the plateau of Chota Nagpur. The Damodar Valley is one of the most industrialised parts of India. Three integrated steel plants (Bokaro, Burnpur and Durgapur) of Steel Authority of India Limited (SAIL) and other factories are located in the valley.

Damodar Valley contains a variety of mineral deposits, including very large deposits of coal and refractory materials. The largest (almost the only) reserves of coking coal in the country are found in the Jharia coalfields in the valley.

The valley also generates 60% of India's medium grade coal. Coal India Limited operates in the valley in a big way. Several dams have been constructed in the valley, for the generation of hydroelectric power. The valley is called "the Ruhr of India". Damodar Valley Corporation, popularly known as DVC, came into being on July 7, 1948 by an Act of the Constituent Assembly of India (Act No. XIV of 1948) as the first multipurpose river valley project of independent India. It is modelled on the Tennessee Valley Authority of the USA.

The initial focus of the DVC were flood control, irrigation, generation, transmission and distribution of electricity, eco-conservation and afforestation, as well as job creation for the socio-economic well being of the people residing in and around areas affected by DVC projects. However, over the past few decades, power generation has gained priority. Other objectives of the DVC, however, remain part of its primary responsibility. The dams in the valley have a capacity to moderate peak floods of 650,000 to 250,000 ft^3/s. DVC has created irrigation potential of 3640 square kilometres.

The first dam was built across the Barakar river, a tributary of the Damodar river at Tilaiya in 1953. The second one was built across the Konar river, another tributary of the Damodar river at Konar in 1955. Two dams across the rivers Barakar and Damodar were built at Maithon in 1957 and Panchet in 1959. Both the dams are some 8 km upstream of the confluence point of the rivers. These four major dams are controlled by DVC. Durgapur barrage was constructed downstream of the four dams in 1955, across the Damodar river at Durgapur in 1955, with head regulators for canals on either side for feeding an extensive system of canals and distributaries.

In 1978, the Government of Bihar (that was before the formation of the state of Jharkhand) constructed the Tenughat dam across the Damodar river outside the control of DVC. It proposes to construct a dam across the Barakar river at Belpahari in Jharkhand state. There are hydro-electric power stations at Tilayia, Maithon and Panchet, with total installed capacity of 144 MW. The one at Maithon was India's first underground hydro-electric power station.

DEMOGRAPHICS

Jharkhand has a population of 26.90 million, consisting of 13.86 million males and 13.04 million females. The sex ratio is 941 females to 1000 males.

The population consists of 28% tribals, 12% Scheduled Castes and 60% others. There are 274 persons for each square kilometre of land.

However, the population density varies considerably from as low as 148 per square kilometre in Gumla district to as high as 1167 per square kilometre in Dhanbad district.

Jharkhand has remained a home to a number of tribal communities since time immemorial. In fact, in some of the districts of Jharkhand, the tribal population predominates, the non tribal one. Jharkhand has 32 primitive tribal groups. These are the Asur, Baiga, Banjara, Bathudi, Bedia, Binjhia, Birhor, Birjia, Chero, Chick-Baraik, Gond, Gorait, Ho, Karmali, Kharwar, Khond, Kisan, Kora, Korwa, Lohra, Mahli, Mal-Paharia, Munda, Oraon, Parhaiya, Santal, Sauria-Paharia, Savar, Bhumij, Kol and Kanwar.

The geographical area now comprising Jharkhand was previously part of Bihar. The area has witnessed migration of people from the adjoining areas of Bihar and West Bengal for last several decades. Industrial and mining centres like Jamshedpur, Dhanbad and Ranchi have attracted people from all parts of India.

Hinduism, Jainism and Buddhism are the native religion while Islam and Christianity were the two religions that came in through immigrants. The tribal communities of Jharkhand have their own spiritual beliefs, commonly called Sarna. During the colonization process the tribal religious beliefs were looked down upon as pagan and inferior. Through overt and covert conversions and other influences at assimilation, the Christian missionaries have contributed much for the demolition of many of the tribal Sarna beliefs.

FOREST PEOPLES PROGRAMME

Since 2002 the World Bank has been trying to promote a Participatory Forest Management (PFM) Project in the newly formed Jharkhand State in India. The hugely controversial Government Eviction Order of May 2002, which generated immediate national and international outrage, did cause the Bank to take a step back.

As a result, progress on project proposals for Jharkhand was stalled as Bank officials sought "dialogue" with the Government of India on how World Bank-assisted projects should deal with so-called "encroachers" in forest areas which the government claims are State property.

Bank officials report that these difficulties have been largely overcome in the case of Jharkhand and a compromise solution for the whole of India is set out in new general guidelines on World Bank engagement with the Forest Sector in India.

However, nobody knows what these guidelines say on the encroachment issue as these principles remain confidential. Bank staff assert that the guidelines will not be available to the public until they are formally "agreed" between the Bank and central government.

The Bank maintains that the forthcoming guidelines are not mandatory, but rather generic principles for deciding eligibility for World Bank loans for forestry projects or forest-related programmes in India.

While these guidelines are being finalised, the Bank has pushed ahead with its plans in Jharkhand. To this end, in mid-July 2004, it gave the green light internally for the implementation of a $2 million (9 Crore Rupees) pilot PFM project in Jharkhand involving 50 villages in five Districts.

At the same time, the Bank gave the go-ahead for 16 months preparation work for the larger State-wide PFM project which is likely to be financed by a $110 million USD loan. The Bank admits that the pilot project has not been formally approved by the Bank's Board of Directors and task managers confirm that this procedure of including actual field pilot projects during project preparation has not been done in any previous World Bank forestry projects in India.

Lack of Transparency in Bank's Plans : Adivasi leaders, activists and civil society organisations in Jharkhand are questioning the whole process by which the pilot phase in Jharkhand has been approved internally by the Bank.

They ask: how have Adivasi organisations, traditional authorities and Gram Sabahs in the 5 affected Districts been consulted?

How has their agreement to the pilot phase been obtained and has such agreement been verified as genuine collective acceptance to the pilot JFM project? As Sanjay Bosu Mullick of Jharkhand Save the Forest Movement explains:

> *"We want to know how exactly was the approval of Adivasi organisations and Gram Sabahs in affected communities were obtained prior to the Bank's public announcement that a pilot JFM initiative is to start as quickly as possible in 5 Districts in Jharkhand. Also, we want to know how the Bank has pushed through this pilot phase before its guidelines on Bank Forestry Projects in India are available to the public. Why are these guidelines still confidential? What are the minimum preconditions for Bank engagement in the forest sector in India? How does the Bank plan to recognise and respect people's rights?"*

At this stage, activists have not even been able to obtain information about which districts will be affected.

For its part, the Bank claims that specific villages have still not been identified, and will be selected on a "demand" basis. However, there is no clarity on how such demand will be judged to be truly coming from the grassroots and to what extent the position of Gram Sabahs and traditional authorities will be respected.

Defective Public Consultations : Over the last few years, World Bank staff have made individual approaches to activists and Adivasi leaders in Ranchi in order to hear their views on the proposed project. Those approached complain that their criticisms of the Bank's plans fall on deaf ears, while the larger public consultations held in Ranchi in November and December 2003 hardly involved any Adivasi representatives critical of the World Bank's plans to support JFM.

The few that did manage to attend complain that the meetings were overwhelmingly attended by NGOs who are eager to secure contracts as facilitators for the World Bank project and by villages that have already accepted JFM committees. A strong rejection of JFM and the opposition to the proposed Bank project was made by a few Adivasi representatives in the workshops, but their interventions were either rejected or ignored. Adivasi leaders and activists therefore protest that World Bank consultations in Jharkhand have been one-sided and have failed to respect dissenting voices.

Flawed and Unjust Project Design: Despite very persuasive and arguably misleading language about "empowerment" and a "people-centred" approach, scrutiny of the Bank's Project Information Document (PID) for the PFM project has alarmed Adivasi leaders and activists in Jharkhand as it proposes an "Action Restriction Process Framework", a "Physical Displacement Policy Framework" as well as "site-specific resettlement Action Plans". Tribal representatives question how the Bank can promote a project that reinforces the states JFM policy which has been widely repudiated by the tribal movement in Jharkhand in both a memorandum to the government in November 2002 and in the Khunti Declaration of November 2003.

Adivasi representatives point out that the Bank is planning to back a forest policy that is not acceptable to tribal communities who live in and depend on Jharkhand's forests. They are dismayed that the World Bank appears to be riding rough-shod over their opposition to the internationally-financed PFM project:

> *"The Bank is planning to finance a forest policy that is not accepted by the vast majority of Adivasi leaders in Jharkhand. The Adivasi people here have clearly stated they do not want JFM, but rather their own genuine*

self-management of their ancestral forests. We challenge the Bank to show us where Adivasi leaders have accepted this specific JFM policy and their project plans? We do not accept Bank projects that reinforce government policies on forests that are rejected by the very people the Bank claims it is seeking to help. Nor do we accept the offering of development benefits, paid work and poverty reduction on the condition that people accept JFM and surrender land to the Forest Department. How can the Bank justify this top-down project?" [Alistair Bodra, Mundari leader and Adivasi activist, Ranchi District, Jharkhand, July 04]

Another Top-down World Bank Project: The World Bank claims it has learned from past mistakes in India and maintains that it would never promote a project that is not broadly accepted by forest-dependent peoples and civil society. Bank officials say that any imposition of an unwanted project would risk promoting public protests that would not be helpful to the Bank nor the Borrower government. Yet in Jharkhand all the signs are that the Bank risks imposing a project that is not wanted by the people.

Meanwhile, in a desperate effort to secure Bank funds the Jharkhand Forest Department is pressuring forest communities to form Village Forest Protection Committees - Vana Samrakshana Samithi (VSS). Forest officials are promising development benefits in return for the formation of such committees. Activists in Jharkhand complain the Forest Department is abusing the people and taking advantage of their poverty to advance their own agenda of appropriating land for plantations and scientific forestry. Yet villagers are not informed of the hidden agenda of the Forest Department and its JFM policy:

"In Hazaribag District the Forest Department has been very active and is all over the place talking to villagers, promising them roads, check-dams and paid work if they accept JFM and allow the Forest Department to

> *work with their village....The people are confused and serious rifts are opening up in village communities over whether or not to accept the JFM committee. Villagers are in desperate poverty and the Forest Department is offering them cash and jobs... But those that have joined the scheme now see their land being lost to plantations. They are beginning to realise that the Forest Department propaganda is not true and does not benefit them!" [Pushpa, JJB Meeting, July 2004]*

In the majority of Adivasi villages where people are more aware of the problems with the state JFM policy, advances by the Forest Department are being strongly opposed.

In response, the government officials have sought to by-pass opposition by creating VSS on paper without collective agreement from the villagers or their authorities. In one case, 10 villages in Southern Ranchi District learned that the forest department had named them as having formed VSS even though there had been no prior consultation in their villages.

On challenging the officials concerned they admitted that they had falsified papers. In this case, after much protest the fraudulent papers were eventually nullified. However, organisations like Jharkhand Save the Forest Movement fear that many more spurious VSS are being established all over Jharkhand:

> *"Jharkhand Jangal Bachao Andolan is challenging the Forest Department's tactics. We are asking them to justify the formation of JFM Committees by methods that avoid the legitimate village authorities of the Gram Sabhas. The Department is maintaining that the Gram Sabha has no say in the formation of the JFM Committees. We reject their position. We maintain that the current underhand methods used by the Forest Department are arguably in violation of the law and that many recently-formed VSS in Jharkhand can be shown*

to be illegal" [Sanjay Bosu Mullick, JJB Meeting, July, 2004]

It still remains to be seen how the World Bank will respond to the legitimate outstanding questions and criticisms of Adivasi peoples and civil society in Jharkhand about its controversial plans to press ahead with support for JFM in the State.

6

Economy

ECONOMY

Open-cast Coal Mining in Dhanbad

Jharkhand has several towns and innumerable villages with civic amenities. Urbanization ratio is 24.1% and the per capita annual income is US$726.8. Jharkhand also has immense mineral resources: minerals ranging from (ranking in the country within bracket) from iron ore(1st), coal(3rd), copper ore (1st), mica (1st), bauxite (3rd), Manganese, limestone, china clay, fire clay, graphite (8th), kainite (1st), chromite(2nd), asbestos (1st), thorium (3rd), sillimanite, uranium (Jaduguda mines, Narwa Pahar) (1st) and even gold (Rakha Mines) (6th) and silverand several other minerals. Large deposits of coal and iron ore support concentration of industry, in centres like Jamshedpur, Dhanbad, Bokaro and Ranchi. Tata Steel, a *S&P CNX 500* conglomerate has its corporate office and main plant in Tatanagar, Jharkhand. It reported a gross income of . 204,910 million for 2005. NTPC will start coal production from its captive mine in state in 2011–12, for which the company will be investing about Rs 1,800 crore.

Agriculture is another sector in economy of Jharkhand which helps economy to grow. In Jharkhand, farmers produce several crops such as rice, wheat, maize, pulses, potatoes, and vegetables such as tomato, carrots, cabbage, brinjal, pumpkin, and papaya. The other Industry are cottage industry and IT industry.

INDUSTRY

Jharkhand has a concentration of some of the country's highly industrialized cities such as Jamshedpur, Ranchi, Bokaro and Dhanbad. It also has several firsts in India, including:

- Largest fertilizer factory of its time in India (since shut down) at Sindri
- First Iron & steel factory at Jamshedpur
- Largest Steel plant in Asia, Bokaro Steel Plant.
- Biggest explosives factory at Gomia
- First methane gas well

On the other hand, it has several towns and innumerable villages with sub-standard civic amenities. Urbanization ratio is only 22.25% and the per capita annual income is only US$ 90.

Jharkhand also has immense mineral resources: minerals ranging from (ranking in the country within bracket) from iron ore (1st), coal (3rd), copper ore (1st), mica (1st), bauxite (3rd), Manganese, limestone, china clay, fire clay, graphite (8th), kainite (1st), chromite (2nd), asbestos (1st), thorium (3rd), sillimanite, uranium (Jaduguda mines, Narwa Pahar) (1st) and even gold (Rakha mines) (6th) and silver and several other minerals.

Large deposits of coal and iron ore support concentration of industry, in centres like Jamshedpur, Bokaro and Ranchi. Tata Steel, a S&P CNX 500 conglomerate has its corporate office in Jharkhand. It reported a gross income of Rs.204,910 million for 2005.

AGRICULTURE

Principal foodgrains crops are paddy, wheat, maize and pulzes.

INDUSTRY AND MINERALS

Jharkhand has the country's two biggest steel plants at Bokaro in the public sector and Tata Iron and Steel Company (TISCO) in Jamshedpur in the private sector. Other important industries are Tata Engineering and Locomotive Company, Sriram Bearing, Usha Martin, Indian Tube Company, etc.

The state is abundantly rich in minerals-copper, coal, iron, manganese, mica, chromite, bauxite, etc., and has the potential of becoming one of the most prosperous states of India.

POWER

The installed capacity of power in Jharkhand is 2,590 MW. This includes 420 MW (Tenughat Thermal Power Station), 840 MW (Patratu Thermal Power Station), 130 MW (Sikkidri Hydel) and 1,200 MW (DVC, Thermal/Hydel). The prospects of capacity addition in both the thermal and hydel sectors of various power stations is 4,736 MW. This includes 686 MW hydel generation.

To provide electricity to all villages and rural areas, the State Government has made a provision of Rs.30 crore during 2001-02.

PFC INVITES RFQ FOR JHARKHAND UMPP

After the successful completion of bidding for Sasan and

Mundra ultra mega power projects (UMPPs), the state-run Power Finance Corporation (PFC) has invited request for qualification (RFQ) for 4,000 mw UMPP in Jharkhand. It has formed a wholly-owned subsidiary, Jharkhand Integrated Power Ltd., for carrying out entire bidding process for the upcoming project.

Bidders are expected to submit RFQs by March 20 while their shortlisting based on responses to RFQ and issuance of request for proposal (RFP) would take place on April 2.

The cut-off date to submit technical and price bids is July 2. PFC plans to shortlist successful bidder and issue letter of intent by July 16 and subsequently sign agreement by September 17.

The power from the upcoming plant would be procured on a competitive bidding route by Delhi, Uttar Pradesh, Punjab, Haryana, Rajasthan, Madhya Pradesh, Gujarat, Maharashtra, Bihar and Jharkhand.

Power Finance Corporation sources told FE the project includes establishment, operation and maintenance of a 4,000 mw coal-fired pit head power project including mine development and transportation of coal from the proposed allocated captive coal mines at North Karanpura. The project site is located near Tilaiya village.

According to request for qualification, the bidders' internal resource generation should be equal to at least Rs 1,140 crore or equivalent to five times the maximum internal resources generated during any of the last five years of business operations.

Bidders should have networth of Rs 1,000 crore and the annual turnover of Rs 2,400 crore. The bidders must meet technical requirement of having experience of developing projects in the last 10 years whose aggregate capital costs must not be less than Rs 3,000 crore.

Out of these projects, the capital cost of at least one project should be equivalent or more than Rs 500 crore.

TRANSPORT

Ranchi Airport (IXR)

National Highway 33 near Ramgarh Cantonment

Air

Ranchi Airport is the largest domestic airport in the state with air connectivity to major Indian cities of Delhi, Kolkata, Bangalore, Mumbai, Hyderabad among others. Other airports present in the state are Bokaro Airport, Jamshedpur Airport, Chakulia Airport, Atal Bihari International Airport, Deoghar, Dumka Airport and Dhanbad Airport who mostly run private and charter flights.

Roads

Jharkhand has extensive network of National Highways and State Highways.

There is 2,661.83 kilometres (1,653.98 mi) of paved National Highways in the state as of 2016.

The National highways present in the state are numbered 2, 6, 23, 31, 32, 33, 43, 75, 78, 80, 98, 99, 100, 114A, 133, 133B, 133A, 143A, 220, 333, 333A, 343 and 419.

The Golden Quadrilateral network of Delhi – Kolkata route runs through Jharkhand notably at Dhanbad.

State Highway 2 in the Mountainous Patratu Valley

Ports

Jharkhand is landlocked state but has numerous rivers and waterways. A multi-model port has been planned at Sahebganj where river Ganges flows. The project is estimated to cost INR 6,500 crores and phase-1 is estimated to be completed by 2019.

Rail

Jharkhand is very well connected by railways and has numerous railway stations.

7

Tourism

TOURISM

Jonha Falls

Jharkhand is known for its waterfalls, hills and holy places. Some tourist spots in State are Hundru Falls, Jonha Falls, Netarhat, Parasnath, Baidyanath Dham, Betla National Park and Dalma Wildlife Sanctuary.

Tourism in Jharkhand refers to tourism in indian state of Jharkhand. The state is famous for its waterfalls, hills and religious shrines. The major religious centre is Deoghar.

Business tourism

Jharkhand is one of the most industrialized states in the country. There are many Indian and global companies located in Jharkhand.

Cruise Tourism

Dimna Lake in Jamshedpur and Ranchi Lake in Ranchi are foumous for cruise in State.

Hill stations

Due to the state located in Chhota Nagpur Plateau, there are several hills in state. Some hills are:

- Netarhat, Latehar district
- Parasnath, Giridih district
- Ranchi Hill, Ranchi
- Trikut, Dumka district
- Canary Hills, Hazaribagh
- Dalma Hill, Jamshedpur
- Sati Hills, Barkagaon, Hazaribagh, The place is known for abnormally large sized caves full of beautiful cave paintings.

Waterfalls of Jharkhand

The are several beautiful waterfalls in state. They are as follows:

- Dassam Falls, Ranchi district
- Hirni Falls, West Singhbhum
- Hundru Falls, Ranchi district
- Jonha Falls, Ranchi district
- Lodh Falls, Latehar district
- Lower Ghaghri Falls, Latehar district

- Panchghagh Falls, Khunti district
- Rajrappa, Ramgarh district
- Sadni Falls, Gumla district
- Usri Falls, Giridih district

Dassam Falls

Wildlife and National Parks

Jharkhand is knows as land of Forest. There are several Wildlife Sanctuaries and National Parks including Betla National Park,, Hazaribag Wildlife Sanctuary, Dalma Wildlife Sanctuary and Gautam Budha Wildlife Sanctuary.

Culture

The state of Jharkhand have rich and vibrant tradition. It is known for its local festival of Karam, Sohrai, Phagua, Tussu, Vaha and Sarhul. There are several folk dance in State including Jhumair, Domkach, Painki, Chhau and Mundari dance, which represent its ancient heritage.

Famous dishes of the state include Chirka roti, Malpua, Pittha, Dhuska, Arsa roti, Dudhauri, Litti Chokha and Panipuri (Gupchup).

Pilgrim Places

Pyramid shaped **Shikhara** *of the temple, Baidyanath Temple*

There several important religious shrines in state. They are as follows:

- Baidyanath Temple, Deoghar
- Shikharji, Parasnath : Shikharji is considered one of the most sacred Jain pilgrimage
- Bhadra Kali Temple, Itkhori, Chatra district
- Chhinnamasta Temple, Rajrappa, Ramgarh district
- Basukinath Temple, Basukinath, Dumka district
- Pahari mandir, Ranchi
- Jagannath Temple, Ranchi
- Aamreshwar Dham Temple, Angrabari, Khunti district
- Trikutachal Mahadeva Temple, Trikut, Dumka district

- Shiv Temple, Mahadevsal, West Singhbhum district
- Shri Shri Ugratara Nagar Mandir, Chandwa, Latehar district

Jal Mandir at Shikharji, Parasnath

Archaeological sites and Heritage

There are several archeological sites in State which are:

- Cave Paintings, Isko, Hazaribagh district
- Megalith Prehistoric Monument, Pakri Barwadih, Hazaribagh district
- Gopalpur Historical Ruins, Dhanbad district
- Archaeological Ruins Of Benisagar, West Singhbhum district
- Palamu Forts, Palamu district
- Navratangarh Fort, Gumla district
- Maluti, Dumka district
- Teliagarhi Fort, Sahibganj District

Part of Palamu Forts

Museums

There are several museums in State which have preserved ancient artifacts discovered from state such as Stone tools, teracotta and sculpture.

- Ranchi Science Centre, Ranchi
- State Museum Hotwar, Ranchi
- Tribal Research Institute and Museum, Ranchi
- Sanskriti Museum & Art Gallery, Hazaribagh

WILDLIFE

Betla National Park: Palamau's Betla National Park offers a fascinating study of wild life in natural surroundings studded with forests, hills and valleys. The national park has a large variety of wild life. Once Betla had 2 tigers, 50 elephants, 800 sambhars, hundreds of wild boar and pythons as big as 15 to 20 feet. Most popular are the spotted deer seen moving in herds. The most coveted sight is a majestic gaur popularly known as bison. The elephants are also seen in the region. The other mammalian fauna to be seen at Betla include langur, rhesus, cheetal (spotted deer), blue bulls and wild boars. The lesser mammals are the porcupine hare junglee cat, honey badger, jackal, malabar giant squirrel and mangoose wolf, antelope etc. The park was declared in 1974 a tiger project reserve.

Maluti Temple terracotta works

Jaivik Udyan (Zoological Park: About 16km from Ranchi town on Ranchi - Patna road near Ormanjhi, is the zoological garden named Jaivik Udyan.

Hazaribagh National Park: Hazaribagh National Park, about 135 km from Ranchi is also a sanctuary adorned with scenic beauties. The park has also the same features as that of Betla to some extent. The park has tigers, panthers, sambhars, spotted deer, bisons and a number of mammalian faunas. There are some towers which the tourists use to behold the beasts. 'Sal' is the dominant tree spices. Wild bear, sambhar, nilgai, chital and kakar are populous. Sloth bears, tigers and panthers also prowl.

Palamau Tiger Reserve: The Palamau Tiger Reserve lies in the western part of the Chhotanagpur plateau. The forest stretches from the edge of the Netarhat hill range in the south to the Auranga river in the north and from the Latehar-Sarju road in the east to Madhya Pradesh border in the west. The forest of Palamau is the catchment of the river North Koel.

Flora includes Shorea robusta, Acacia catechu, Butea monosperma, Madhuca indica, Terminalia tomentosa, Pterocarpus marsupium, Adina cardifolia, Anogeisus latifolia, Indigofera pulchela, Moghania spp, Mallotus phillipinensis, Holarrhena antidysentrica, Bothriochloa montana, Apluda mutica and many others. Fauna includes Tiger, Leopard, Cheetal, Sambar, Barking Deer, Wolf, Wild Dog, Elephant, Mouse Deer, Pangolin, Fourhorned Antelope and Indian Ratel.

Topchanchi Wildlife Sanctuary: This sanctuary is noted for the flow of migratory birds including pochards, red crested pochards and coots. Resident birds include bronze winged jacanas, pond herons, egrets, swamp partridges, etc. The Nagi Dam Sanctuary (1.9sq km) near Jhajha is the smallest sanctuary in the state and also a place to spot migratory birds. 15km from Patna, Danapur is also a significant shelter for migratory birds, especially janghils (open billed storks).

Palamu National Park: Palamau on the Auranga river, 20 miles south-east of Daltonganj as the crow flies, from which the district takes its name is for historian and archaeologist the most interesting place in the district, for it was for many years the seat of the Chero chiefs and it contains the ruins of the two great forts built by them, the capture of which by Mughals and later by the British resulted in the collapse of the Chero resistance, the forts lie within the reserved forests and in order to preserve them the jungle has to be cut back at intervals they are a favourite haunt of tigers, whose pug marks may nearly always be seen in and around the fort. The walls which are in preservation are about 5 feet in thickness and those of the old fort bear marks of cannon balls and bullets in many places. In the new fort the Nagpuri gate is of great beauty.

It is said to have been imported of great expense by Medni Roy, the greatest of the Rajas of "Palamau", after he had sacked the place of the Maharaja of Chhotanagpur ; but the side of the fort on which it was erected was declared to be unlucky, and the entrance was bricked up, the carving being left where it was. The gate has now been opened and some of the adjoining masonry has been demolished in order to preserve it. The following account is taken from the Report of the Archeological Survey, Bengal Circle in 1903-1904 : " There are two forts at Palamau, inside the jungle, close to each other. They are distinguished by the name of Purana Kila and Naya Kila, although the both appear to be of about the same age.

The style of the walls and buildings so closely resembles that at Rohtashgarh and Shergarh that both forts may safely be put down at the same time, *viz.*, the beginning of Mughal period. The old fort is of regular shape, about one mile in circumference. The ground upon which it stands rises in terraces, the higher part is divided from the lower one by a cross wall. The walls are in places of considerable thickness, about 8' the path way on top between the battlements measuring 5'- 6". In other places they are thinner.

The four gates are strongly fortified with inner and outer courts and provided with watch towers. The outer battlements of the walls are loop-holed. Inside are the remains of for two-storied houses and mosque with three domes. The inner cross wall has one gate, in front of which is a deep well cut out of the rocks with a vaulted tunnel leading down to it. The walls are built of stones and concrete, like those at Rohtashgarh and Shergarh.

The houses are plastered over and remains of paintings and stucco ornamentation are seen here and there,. In all these respects, the buildings closely agree with those in the other hill forts, already referred to. I observed one statue of Buddha close to the eastern gate and another broken Hindu or Buddhist idol, but no temple was found by me. The new fort is built around the slopes of a conical hill. There are two lines of walls. Each making up a square. The inner line clusters around the peak of the hill ; the outer line is somewhat lower down. The walls are of the same kind as in the old fort.

The outer walls are of considerable breadth, the passage along the roof between the battlements measuring 14' and the total breadth amounting to 18'.there are no separate building inside the enclosure, but the walls have galleries, open to the interior, sometimes of several stories.

The most interesting object is fine stone-carved window about 15'high. There is nothing to match this either at Rohtasgarh or Shergarh. The carving is distinctly of the Mughal type. Another similar window close to it is broken and some wall near it also have fallen down and now block up the passage so that it is difficult to get a view of this excellent piece of carving". The above note still holds good.

Palamau is now often mistaken as Palamau District. It may be mentioned here that the East India Gazetteer by Walter Hamilton (1815) has the following description. If this district:--"A hilly and jungly district in the province of Jharkhand, situated between the 23rd and 25th degrees of north latitude.

This is one of the least cultivated and most thinly inhabited territories in the Company's dominions, a great proportion of the land consisting of hills covered with jungle. The soil in many parts is strongly impregnated with iron.

HAZARIBAGH NATIONAL PARK

About Hazaribagh National Park: Nestling in low hilly terrain, at an average altitude of 615 meters in the Indian state of Jharkhand, the Hazaribagh National Park has an abundance of wild animals like the wild boar, sambar, nilgai, chital, sloth bear, tiger and panther.

Visiting Hours (Hazaribagh National Park) : The climate in this region is tropical with hot summers and cold winters. Temperature during the summer months touch a high of 41.1'C and a low of 19.4'C. Winter months are better and the temperature ranges between a maximum and minimum of 19.4'C and 7'C. The monsoon months are July to mid-September.

How To Get There (Hazaribagh National Park)

Air : The nearest airport Ranchi (91 km) is connected with Calcutta, Patna, Lucknow and Delhi by regular Indian Airlines flights.

Rail : The nearest railway station is Koderma, which is 59 km away, or alternately one can approach the park from the Hazaribagh Road railway station (67 km) on the Howrah-Delhi Grand Chord line.

Road : Hazaribagh town is connected by road to Ranchi 91 km, Dhanbad 128 km, Gaya 130 km, Patna 235 km, Daltongunj 198 km, and Calcutta (via Asansol-Govindapur-Barhi) 434 km. The Hazaribagh National Park is 19 km from the Hazaribagh town. Regular bus services connect the town with Koderma, Hazaribagh Road railway station, Patna, Gaya, Ranchi, Dhanbad, Daltongunj and other nearby places.

Internal Transport (Hazaribagh National Park): Unmetered Taxis, Auto Rickshaws, Cycle Rickshaws and Taxis are available for the park from the Hazaribagh town. The approximate charge for a taxi is Rs. 160 for a two-way journey.

Attractions (Hazaribagh National Park) : Sighting of wild boar, sambar, nilgai, cheetal, and kakar is assured especially near the waterholes at dusk. Tigers being less in number-14 according to the 1991 census-are difficult to sight. The sanctuary stretches over 184 square km of undulating country and steep hills with dense tropical forests and grass meadows.

A 111-km road in the sanctuary takes motorists to the remotest corners and to masonry towers. Strategically located, the road offers excellent opportunities for viewing the wilds. The sanctuary is surrounded by tribal habitation. There are many watchtowers that provide perfect hideouts to see the wildlife in its true natural habitat.

Places Around (Hazaribagh National Park): The Palamau Forest Reserve is another major wildlife sanctuary in the region. Places of the tourist interest in the vicinity include Canari Hill-5 km, Rajrappa-Falls 89 km, and Suraj Kund hot spring-72 km.

Travel Tips (Hazaribagh National Park) : A trip to the park starts at 1700 hours from the Divisional Forest Office, West Division, Hazaribagh and it ends at 2200 hours. Charges are Rs.50 per head. Reservation can be made with the Divisional Forest Officer, West Division, Hazaribagh.

BETLA NATIONAL PARK

Situated in the district of Daltonganj, Palamau Sanctuary is spread over an area of 979 sq. km. The core area of 232 sq. kms of the sanctuary was declared as Betla National park in September 1989. The park occupies the western parts of the Chhotanagpur plateau and was constituted in the year 1960 as an extension of the Hazaribagh National park. Palamau has the distinction of being the forest where the world's first tiger census was enumerated in 1932. The park became one of the earliest 9 tiger reserves in India under 'Project Tiger' in 1974.

The forests of the park have a vast range of vegetation consisting of tropical wet evergreen forests in the lower reaches, mixed (moist & dry) deciduous forests in the middle and temperate alpine forests in the upper reaches including Sal and bamboo as the major components along with a number of medicinal plants.

The river Koel and its tributaries run through the northern portion of the park. There are grasslands in the river flowing area. It has waterfalls and hot springs too. Once the seat of Chero kings, there are two historical forts, one of them belonging to the 16th century deep inside the forest. The main sentinel of the old fort is visible high up on the hill with defences in three directions and three main gates.

The diversity of eco-system promotes a wide variety of fauna consisting of elephant, panther, leopard, wild boar, tiger, gaur, sloth bear, sambar, chital, nuntjac, nilgai, langur, mouse deer, monkeys, small Indian civet, mongoose, jackals, porcupine, ant eating pangolin etc.

Elephants in large numbers are seen mostly during the monsoons up to the time when water sources begin to dry up in March. Jackal and hyena are common scavengers. Bird-life is rich featuring the hornbill, peafowl, red jungle fowl, black partridge, white necked stork, black ibis, swamp grey, quail, the pied born bill, wagtails, the harial, doves, drongo, the crested serpent-eagle, forest owls, the papiha and other birds usually found in dry deciduous forests. The famous Kamaldah lake attracts several varieties of water birds including the common whistling and cotton teal, the comb duck, snipe and geese. The rhesus monkey and the common languor provide attraction to children visiting the park.

Described as one of the finest parks in the north-east for observing a variety of wild life from close range, there are elephant rides and jeeps available with guides and spotlight for venturing inside the park. Watch towers and ground hides have been constructed to view the wild life.

TOURIST ATTRACTIONS

Dassam Falls: About 40 km. away from Ranchi on Tata Road falls a village named Taimara near which flows the Kanchi river, Falling from a height of about 144 feet Kanchi river makes a pretty fall called Dassam falls known as Dassam Ghagh also encircled with charming scences. The tourists are warned not to take bath in the falls or at least be careful while bathing in the stream.

Hundru Falls: Ranchi is nature's bounty to mother India which has specially been adorned with falls and streams. Hundru falls is about 28 km. aways from Ranchi town. The Swarnarekha river falls from a height of 320 feet making a wonderful scene known as Hundru falls. During rainy season it takes a formidable form but in summer it turns into an exciting picnic spot.

Jonha Falls: Jonha is about 40 km. away from Ranchi. The road leading to Jonha is a bit narrow but not so rough and rugged as well as arduous as that of Hundru. There is also a hospice Tourists rest house which accommodates Lord Gautam Budha's temple. This falls is named after Gautam as Gautamdhara too, it is approachable by road. The tourists can go upto Gautamdhara station by train also.

Hirni Falls: About 70 km. From Ranchi on way to Chakradharpur is located Hirni Falls. Having situated amidst dense forest Hirni has been favoured by nature for scenic beauties. The tourists are carried away by emotions and flight of imagination while observing Hirni.

Ranchi Hill: Ranchi, being situated at an altitude of 21,40 feet from sea level, is a popular health and holiday resort and a place of sacred pilgrimate. Some comely sights in the town include Ranchi Hill, Tagore Hill, Ranchi Lake etc. A panoramic view of the town can be behond from the hill top. The Shiva Temple situated on the top of the hill, is an added attraction for the devotees for whom it assumes the places of reverence during Shravanmas same as that of Baijnath Dham (Deoghar).

Jamshedpur: Named after Jamshedji Tata, where the foundation of Indian Steel Industry was laid.

Gonda Hill and Rock Garden: About 4 km. from G.P.O., Ranchi on Kanke Road, just in fornt of the CMPDIL Hq. Is situated the Gonda Hill with a water reservoir at its top. At the foot of the hill is a big lake known as Kanke Dam and a lucrative place for tourists.

Tagore Hill: About 3 km. from the Ranchi G.P.O. the Tagore Hill is about 300 ft. high. As the hill is associated with a history pertaining to Tagore family, it is known as Tagore Hill. A number of books are supposed to have been written by Rabindra Nath Tagore on the top of the hill. At the foot of the hill are situated the Ramakrishna Mission Ashram and its office and centre of Divyayan and agrarian vocational institute.

Jagannathpur Temple and Hill: About 10 km. From Ranchi G.P.O. is another sight seeing place where the tourists can rejoice and worship. The old temple of lord Jagannath, built in 1691 in the architectural style of Puri Temple stands like a fort on the top of the in the hill. Its car/chariot festival held light part on Ashadhmas draws a big crowd comprising of tribals and non-tribals. HEC township nearby is an added attraction.

Angrabadi: Angrabadi is actually, a temple complex which accommodates the temples of Lords Ganpati, Ram-Sita and Hanuman and Shiva. The Shankracharya Swami Swarupanand Saraswati, having been captivated by serene, placid and celestial beauty of Angrabadi rechristened it as Amreshwar Dham.

Sun Temple: About 39 km. from Ranchi on Tata Road near Bundu stands on the desolate bush green the elegant Sun temple fashioned in the form of huge chariot with richly decorated 18 wheels and seven life like horses ready to take of. Built by Sanskrit Vihar headed by Shri Ram Maroo, the managing director of Ranchi Express, the sun temple deserves the title "a poem in stone". The surroundings of the temple are studded with a pond serving as a sacred place for Chhathavratis.

Netarhat: Popularly called the 'Queen of Chhotanagpur' Netarhat is 154 km west of Ranchi Town. It is a plateau covered with thick forests situated at a height of 3,700 feet or 1128 metres. Generally people visit this place to enjoy the breath taking Sunrise and Sunset.

Hazaribagh: Nestling in low hilly terrain, at an average altitude of 1800 ft. (615 metres) this 183.89 sq. kms National Park has an abundance of wild animals, *i.e.* wild Boar, Sambar, Nilgai, Chital, Sloth Bear, tiger and Panthar. The 1970 census has established the presence of 14 tigers, 25 Panthers and 400 Sambars.

Baidyanath Dham (Deoghar): Baidyanath Dham situated in the Santhal Parganas of Jharkhand, is a very important piligram Centre. It's famous for the Hindus for the temple of Shiva-Baidyanath and the place is a popular holiday Centre.

Panchet: Famous for Panchet Dam. It is constructed on Damodar river, is 22,155 ft. long and 124 ft. high. A hydel station has also been constructed against the back ground of Panchet Hill in the eastern side of dam.

Maithon: Famous Maithon Dam is situated here. Maithon can also be translated as "Mother's Abode". Maithon has the biggest reservoir in the Damodar Valley Corporation.

Topchanchi: Famous for beautiful artificialy created lake, the Topchanhci lake lies 37 km from Dhanbad and is almost on NH_2.

Parasnath: The highest hill in Jharkhand, towering to an elevation of 4480 feet. The Parasnath Temple is considered to be one of the most important and sanctified holy places of the Jains. According to Jain tradition, no less than 23 out of 24 Tirthankaras (including Parsvanatha) are believed to have attained salvation here.

Dhanbad: Dhanbad is one of the most important industrial centres in India. In and around Dhanbad is the richest mineral wealth of India. It has the Central Mining Research Station, the Central Fuel Reaserch Institute, the Directorate General of Mines Safety and the Mining College. Other places of importance in Dhanbad are:

Jharia : Suburts of Dhanbad, is rich colliery centre & has entensive commerce.

Sindri : Fertiliser & other factories & Bihar Institute of Technology.

PALAMAU

Palamau is a district of Jharkhand state, India. The district lies between 23°50' and 24°8' north latitude and between 83°55' and 84°30' east longitude. It is bordered on the north by river Son and Bihar, on the east by districts of Chatra and Hazaribagh, on the south by Latehar District and on the west by Garhwa District.

The district covers an area of 5043 square kilometers and has a population of 1,533,176.

Daltonganj, situated on North Koel river in the district headquarters. The town is named after Colonel Dalton, Commissioner of Chhota Nagpur in 1861.

Palamau National Park: The district is home to the famous Palamau National Park known for its wild life. The park is spread over a core area of 250 square kilometers. The area is rich in flora and fauna but also prone to severe droughts. The Palamau National Park was brought under Project Tiger in the year 1973 and is among the original Tiger Reserves of India. Sal and bamboo are the main vegetation.

World's first tiger-census was done in the Palamau forests in the year 1932. Counting was based on pugmarks. There were around 44 tigers when the last census was done. There are several other wildlife found in the sanctuary - chital, chinkara, common langur, dhole (wild dogs), elephants, gaur, hares, Indian porcupine, nilgai, monkey, mouse deer, leopard, pangolin, panther, sambar, sloth bear, wild boar and wolves. Peafowl, red junglefowl and partridges are the common birds found here. The tourists can drive through dense patches of sal and bamboo in the park. A guide and jeep can be hired from the forest department. Watch towers are there to observe the wildlife in relative safety. There are tree houses which can be rented out for stay and food arrangement is also there.

The wildlife sanctuary can be reached by train from Daltonganj or by air from Ranchi

DUMKA

Dumka is a city and a municipality in and headquarters of Dumka district in the state of Jharkhand, India.

Origin of Name: Dumka derives its name from a Persian word damin-i-koh, which means 'skirts (an edge, border or extreme part) of the hills'. The Mughals assigned this name to this and nearby areas on account of presence of hillocks and undulating terrain.

History: Dumka is also the head-quarter of the Northern Evangelical Lutheran Church (NELC), which is especially important among the santal people in the district. This headquarters also administer a lot of property in West Bengal and Assam. Mornai Tea Estate in Goalpara, Assam is a particularly important industry for the economy of the NELC.

Geography: Dumka is located at 24.27° N 87.25° E. It has an average elevation of 137 metres (449 feet). The birth place of Ram keshri.

Demographics: As of 2001 India census GR India, Dumka had a population of 44,917. Males constitute 54% of the population and females 46%. Dumka has an average literacy rate of 76%, higher than the national average of 59.5%: male literacy is 80% and, female literacy is 71%. In Dumka, 12% of the population is under 6 years of age.

Politics: Its first Chief Minister was Babulal Marandi, previously an MP from Dumka district. Sibu Soren is another familiar controversial leader.

Education: The town has very good colleges and schools. S.P. College leads the pack and offers graduation in social science, pure science, economics, mathematics and other subjects. It also has a polytechnic and an ITI but unfortunately no engineering, medical or dental college, so those who wish to pursue a career in these subjects have to move out of the city. It has a very good school St Joseph's High School situated 8 km from Dumka, a place called Guhiajori. This school is surrounded by mountains. This school has excellent academic facilities and a nice garden in front of it. This school is considered as the one of the best school in south Bihar. Many hokey and football players emerge from here.

MAYURAKSHI RIVER

Mayurakshi River (also called Mor River) is a major river in West Bengal, India, with a long history of devastating floods.

It has its source on Trikut hill, about 16 km from Deoghar in Jharkhand state. It flows through Jharkhand and then through the districts of Birbhum and Murshidabad in West Bengal before flowing into the Bhagirathi River. The river is about 250 km long.

Mayurakshi literally means the eye of a peacock (Mayur/ Mor=peacock, Akshi = eye). Mayurakshi though named after its crystal clear water of the dry seasons, floods its valley during the monsoons. Even after the construction of the Massanjore dam, it wreaks havoc with its floods, washing away embankments.

Floods and their Control: The Mayurakshi is famous for its strong current. For seven or eight months in the year the river is a desert - sands stretching from shore to shore for a mile and a half. But when the rains come, she is terrible, demoniac. She races along, four to five miles wide, her deep grey water swamping everything within reach. Then comes once in a while the Harpa flood, when the water, six to seven cubits deep, rushes into villages nearby and washes away homes and granaries and all else in its way. This does not happen very often though. The last time was about twenty years ago.

Many of the rivers that originate on the Chota Nagpur Plateau and flow down into West Bengal are rain fed and have for ages wrought havoc with their seasonal floods. This includes the Mayurakshi. Annual rainfall over the basin varies between 765 and 1607 mm with an average of 1200 mm of which 80% occurs during the monsoon season from June to September.

Some of the historically important floods in this river were recorded by L.S.S. O'Malley in the Bengal District Gazetteers for the districts of Murshidabad and Birbhum. For the district of Birbhum, O'Malley has noted "in 1787 there was a high flood which it is said, in some places swept off villages, inhabitants and cattle, the crops on the ground, with everything that was moveable." O'Malley also recorded that "in 1806 the Mayurakshi and Ajay had a sudden extraordinary rise and floods washed away whole villages." In September 1902, because of heavy rains the Brahmani and the Mayurakshi overflowed their banks and inundated the surrounding country in some places to the depth of 12 to 20 ft.

MASSANJORE DAM

From the counterpart rupee fund created through supplies of wheat and other materials from Canada for use in India, Canada devoted those rupees to the further development of the Mayurakshi dam project. The Massanjore dam (also called Canada Dam), across the Mayurakshi, was commissioned in 1955. It was formally inaugurated by Lester B. Pearson, Foreign Minister of Canada. Unfortunately, the Massanjore dam located near Dumka in the state of Jharkhand (erstwhile Bihar) was not allowed to have any flood reserve. Simultaneously with construction of dams the state government in 1956, selectively took over flood control embankments till then maintained by the landlords or local bodies. Massanjore dam is about 65 km upstream from Siuri in West Bengal. It is 155 feet high from its base and is 2170 feet long. The reservoir has an area of

16,650 acres when full and has a storage capacity of 500,000 acre feet. It had cost Rs. 16.10 crore.

TILPARA BARRAGE

Apart from the Massanjore Dam there is a barrage, some 32 km downstream, at Tilpara, near Siuri. The barrage is 1,013 feet long and had cost Rs. 1.11 crore.

Floods since Then: In the four decades between 1960 and 2000 only five years could be identified as flood free years, when only less than 500 sq kms of area were inundated. After major floods in 1978, West Bengal suffered consecutively in 1998, 1999 and 2000. In 1978, seventy two hours of continuous and concentrated rainfall over the western river basin areas of the Bhagirathi *viz.* from the Pagla-Bansloi to the Ajay, generated so huge flood volume that all embankments on the eastern side of the Bhagirathi were almost washed away and the whole of Nadia district, a larger part of Murshidabad district and northern areas of North 24 Parganas district were flooded and remained underwater for a long period of time. Construction of embankments is the only structural measure available for the provision of relief to the people. Major embankments line long stretches of such rivers as Mayurakshi, Dwarka, Brahmani and Ajay

Irrigation and Power: Massanjore dam has ensured irrigation of some 600,000 acres of land with an estimated resultant increased yield of approximately 400,000 tons of food annually and generation of 2,000 kW of electric power.

JAMTARA

Jamtara is a city and a notified area in Jamtara district in the Indian state of Jharkhand. Jamtara town is the district headquarters.

Its name originated from two words in the local tribal language, Jama (Santhali for Snake) and Tar (Settlement/ Residence) - meaning this area may have been heavily infested with snake. In Mihijam, the other big town in the district, has some of the best doctors in the region for snake bite.

Geography: Jamtara is located at 23.95° N 86.8° E. It has an average elevation of 155 metres (508 feet).

It is located 200 km from Ranchi, the state capital. It has an area of 1801 km^2.

Other towns in this district are Nala, Kundahit, Narayanpur and Fatehpur. As part of the economically backward Santhal Pargana area, this district too has not seen much development. In mineral rich Jharkhand, this is one of the districts with no minerals. As a result, employment is low. Add to it the fact that majority of the land in this area is non sellable (a geriatric law from British times), resulting in no outside investement.

Demographics: As of 2001 India census GR India, Jamtara had a population of 22,426. Males constitute 52% of the population and females 48%. Jamtara has an average literacy rate of 66%, higher than the national average of 59.5%: male literacy is 75%, and female literacy is 57%. In Jamtara, 13% of the population is under 6 years of age.

BOKARO

Bokaro is one of the twenty-two districts of Jharkhand state, India. It was created in the year 1991 by carving out one subdivision consisting of two blocks from Dhanbad District and six blocks from Giridih District. It covers a geographical area of 2861 square kilometres. The average altitude of the land is 210 metres from mean sea level.

The district has a maze of valleys and sub-valleys formed by the River Damodar and its tributaries. They form an important source of water for the industries and townships which have sprung up on it banks in the last few decaded. Some hills and hillocks rise above the gentle valley making it a panoramic landscape to view.

Bokaro Steel City is the district headquarters with a population of around 800,000. The population is drawn from all parts of India. The population is well educated and urbane. Bokaro district has a large steel plant, Bokaro Steel Plant, controlled by Steel Authority of India Limited and several other medium and small industries. The district has already emerged prominently on the industrial map of India. This city is very neat and clean city. The atmosphere of this city is really good.

Lying along the Damodar River, just west of one of India's largest iron and steel plants, along the Dhanbad Ranchi highway is India's biggest steel complex. The Plant was conceived as the country's first Swadeshi Steel Plant to be built with maximum indigenisation going into the equipments, materials and know-how. Thus, this project has been a radical shift from the earlier dependence on foreign sources for know-how and consultancy, design and equipment, supervision, erection, etc. to almost a full measure of self-reliance and confidence.

Situated in the Chhotanagpur Plateau, the vast rolling topography of the city is typical, strewn by graded valleys and winding streams. In this setting, within a short period of two decades, a new city with a strong multi-dimensional economic base, has blossomed into a regional urban centre of around 8.0 lakh people drawn from different parts of the country, giving the city the character of Mini India.

Prime Sites

Bokaro Steel City: As the fourth integrated steel plant in the Public Sector, Bokaro Steel City was conceived in 1959. Bokaro Steel Plant actually started taking shape in 1965 with the collaboration of the then United Sovereign Of Soviet Republic. Major coalfields are located nearby. Bokaro City was built to provide housing and other community facilities for the plant's employees.

Garga Dam And Parasnath Hills: Bokaro City is located in picturesque surroundings on the southern bank of river Damodar with Garga, one of its tributaries meandering along the southern and eastern outskirts of the city. On the north, the city is flanked by the high ranges of the Parasnath Hills and on the south just beyond the river Garga, it is enveloped by the Satanpur hillocks.

Bokaro Ispat Pustakalaya: Located near Bokaro Niwas, it has a collection of over 40,000 books that meets the reading requirements of the people in the township.

City Park: Bokaro has a well-maintained City Park with an artificial lake. Recently three artificial islands have also been created.

Jawaharlal Nehru Biological Park: A Biological Park named after Jawaharlal Nehru with a variety of animals and birds and a modern aquarium is another attraction located in sector 5.

Babudih : A village in Chas Block famous for 75 feet high tower.

Chandrapura : A town famous for Chandrapura Thermal Power Station.

Tenu Ghat: Headquarters of Bermo Sub-Division famous for Tenughat Dam and Tenughat Thermal Power Station.

How to get there

Air: There is no direct air connection but SAIL is having a private air belt at Bokaro.

Rail: Bokaro is near Dhanbad, which is on the main Delhi-Howrah railway line.

Road: Well connected with all the major cities by good motorable roads.

DEOGHAR

Deoghar is headquarters of Deoghar District in the state of Jharkhand, India.

Origin of Name: Deoghar is a Hindi word and the literal meaning of 'Deoghar' is abode ('ghar') of the Gods and Goddesses ('dev'). The place, also known as Baidyanathdham, is a very famous Hindu pilgrimage centre. The Ravneshwar Shiva temple of Deoghar, is a Siddha Peeth and one amongst the twelve Shiva Jyothirlingams in India. The Lingam enshrined here is also known as 'Kamna Lingam'.

Geography: Deoghar is located at 24.48° N 86.7° E. It has an average elevation of 254 metres (833 feet).

Deoghar, the town, has a picturesque location. To the north of the town there is a wood called Data Jungle after a fakir; to the north-west is a low wooded hill called Nandan Pahar; and to the east about 10 miles away there is a low range of hills known as Tiur or Trikutaparvata.

There are a number of small hills to the south-east, south and southwest. There are two rivulets Yamunajor and Dharua near the town. The countryside around Deoghar has an attractive set-up with undulations, water courses and small hills.

The climate is dry and congenial and Deoghar is still considered a health resort in spite of the great congestion particularly due to the temple of Baidyanath and the location of the criminal and civil courts and a very large number of Government establishments.

The nearest railway station is Baidyanathdham. Jasidih junction is about 7 km from Baidyanathdham railway station, which is on the main line of Howrah-Delhi route of Indian railway. It is about 223 km from Patna.

This place is famous for the mela of Shrawan (a Hindu month). Approx. 10-20 lakhs worshipers come with holy water of Ganga from Sultangunj to present it to Shiva, which is almost 104 km from Deoghar. The human unbroken line of 104 km in red dress can been seen here in this month.

Places of Interest in/around Deoghar

Navlakha Temple

Nandan Pahar: This is a small hill edging the town which hosts a famous Nandi Temple. It has been beautifully maintained by the local administration and speaks volume about the beauty of this place. This hill faces the famous Shiv temple on its one side and on the other side it has a beautifull lake luring the visitors.

Basukinath (43 km), where an attractive Shiva temple is located. Satsanga Ashram, a holy place for devotees of Shri Shri Anukul Chandra Thakur. This place can be termed on the lines of great Ashramas. It also holds a zoo in its vicinity which attracts quite a lot of kids and grown ups to it. If one is looking for some time in peace, this is the place to be in.

'Come o traveller, i wait for thee,

feel my tranquility, and purge your pains'

Navalakha Mandir (2 km) where temples of Radha and Krishna stand majestically

Trikut (24 km), where several sages are reputed to have attained salvation. Now this is going to have Jharkhand's first Ropeway.

Demographics: As of 2001 India census GR India, Deoghar had a population of 98,372. Males constitute 55% of the population and females 45%. Deoghar has an average literacy rate of 76%, higher than the national average of 59.5%: male literacy is 82% and, female literacy is 69%. In Deoghar, 12% of the population is under 6 years of age.

Education

Ramakrishna Mission Vidyapith : It is one of the premier schools of eastern India. Known for its calm, serene and pious atmosphere, it has often been referred as an Oasis in the desert.

GIRIDIH

Giridih is headquarters of the Giridih district of Jharkhand state, India. The literal meaning of Giridih is the land of hills & hillocks - giri, a Hindi word, means hills and dih, another word of the local dialect, indicates upland. Giridih district was earlier a part of Hazaribagh district.

Geography: Giridih is located at 24.18° N 86.3° E. It has an average elevation of 289 metres (948 feet).

Nearby Places: Giridih has several interesting spots, including the following:

Usri Falls (13 km)

Khandoli (8km) - a famous picnic spot.

Baidadih, with a well with water reputed to contain several minerals.

Parasnath Hills and Sammet Shikharji, with the highest mountain peak in Jharkhand, 4480 feet above the sea level, it is one of the most important and sanctified holy places of the Jains. 20 out of 24 Tirthankaras (including Parshva) are believed to have attained salvation there.

Kabir Gyan Mandir—abode to Mother Gyan, a disciple of Shri Vivek Prabhujee. There, one can get spiritual enlightenment by participating in religious discources and other functions. Recently, the temple named Guru Govind Dham has come up here over the monumnet of Shri Vivek Prabhujee.

Kharagdiha, a place near Mirjaganj, in close proximity to Giridih, is the abode to the famous saint named Langtababa. He is revered both by the Hindus and the Muslims alike. His samadhi is also located at Kharagdiha.

Demographics: As of 2001 India census GR India, Giridih had a population of 98,569. Males constitute 53% of the population and females 47%. Giridih has an average literacy rate of 69%, higher than the national average of 59.5%: male literacy is 74%, and female literacy is 63%. In Giridih, 15% of the population is under 6 years of age.

Notable Personalities: Sir Jagadish Chandra Bose spent his last days in Giridih and the Sir J.C. Bose Girl's High School is named in his honour. He died in Giridih.

The great literary figure Rabindranath Tagore also had been a resident of Giridih. He wrote his Shivaji Utsav in 1904 at Giridih. His then resident Dawasika Bhawan is still existing at Giridih.

The father of statics, the great Mathematician Prasanta Chandra Mahalanobis was born here. R. K. Mahila College is being run in the house of the red-letter personality of India. Giridih is the headquarters of eastern region of National Sample Survey Organization (NSSO), a Government of India organization on statistics.

Economy: This town used to bustle with economic activity in the period from 60s to 80's when the mineral mica processing and export community reaped tremendous gains through exports to the USSR. Since the decline of the USSR however and its split into twelve CIS countries the industry has slowly declined and is currently ailing.

Education: The major educational institutions in the town include :

Saraswati Shishu/Vidya Mandir- Affiliated to the C.B.S.E. board, this school provides education up to an equivalent of the 10th Standard.

Carmel School - Affiliated to the I.C.S.E board, this school provides education up to an equivalent of the 10th Standard. A co-ed institution, it was founded in 1954 and recently celebrated its 50th year. An Association of the alumni of this school, EXCA was founded some years ago.

D.A.V. BNS Public School - Affiliated to the C.B.S.E board, this school provides co-educational facilities to the children of the community up to XIIth standard. The school has recently moved to a newly built campus. The building was generously donated by J.K. Saha in the fond memory of his grandfather Late Shri Badri Narayan Saha.School has done tremendous progress under very dedicated teachers such as K.K. Dubey sir, Desmukh sir, Mahendra sir, Paul sir, Dutta sir and the list is still long. Subhash Public School in giridih is the biggest boarding school in Jharkhand, this school was started by Late Dr. Param Hand Singh this school is growing in good speed and imparting education to all, affiliated to CBSE up 10+2. Besides the above three major institutions there are other public and private schools as well. The colleges in this town include—The Mahila College for Women The Giridih College affiliated to the Vinobha Bhawe University. One more institution that is helping to bring good quality education is CCL DAV Public School, beniadih.

DHANBAD

Dhanbad is a city and a municipality in Dhanbad district in the state of Jharkhand, India. It is the district headquarters and famous for its coal mines and industrial establishments; because of this, it has been called the "Coal Capital" of India and the "City of Coal." Until October 25, 1956 Dhanbad was a part of Manbhum District, West Bengal.

The Indian School of Mines, located in Dhanbad, draws students from all over India, as well as some other countries. The Central Mining Research Institute (CMRI), and the Central Fuel Research Institute (CFRI), both of which are controlled by the Council of Scientific and Industrial Research (CSIR), are located in the area. The economy of Dhanbad is mainly dependent upon coal and coal based industries. Dhanbad is on the route of the Shatabdi Express, Rajdhani Express.

Tata Steel has set up mines in the area. Coal washing and coke making are the main coal related industry in the city. Other major companies having a presence in the mining activities of this city are :IISCO (Indian Iron And Steel Company), BCCL (Bharat Coking Coal Ltd.). BCCL a subsidiary of the CCL (Coal India Ltd.) is the largest operator of steel mines in this area and has mostly open cast mines, whereas Tata Steel has mostly underground mines. These companies have developed townships for its employees containing roads, water, power and sanitation facilities.

The maximum temperature in winter is 22°C, and the minimum is 8°C. In summer, the maximum is 42°C, and the minimum is 22°C.

Geography: Dhanbad is located at 23.8° N 86.45° E. It has an average elevation of 222 metres (728 feet).

Demographics: As of 2001 India census GR India, Dhanbad had a population of 198,963. Males constitute 54% of the population and females 46%. Dhanbad has an average literacy rate of 74%, higher than the national average of 59.5%: male literacy is 79% and, female literacy is 68%. In Dhanbad, 12% of the population is under 6 years of age.

8

Population and Religion

POPULATION OF JHARKHAND

Jharkhand is a state located in east India and it was removed out of the southern piece of Bihar on 15 November 2000. The state bestows its outskirt with Bihar, UP, Chhattisgarh and West Bengal toward the east. Ranchi is the capital while Jamshedpur is the most swarmed city of the state. The past province of Bihar was parceled into two distinct states of Bihar and Jharkhand.

Cold Weather Season occurs from November to February while summer starts from March to mid-June. Jharkhand has a couple of innumerable towns with civic amenities. Urbanization extent is 24.1% and the per capita yearly wage is US$726.8. The state has a novel old world appeal which is exceptional in its own way.

According to 2011, Jharkhand had a population of 32.96 Million. Statistics information since 1881 has demonstrated a continuous decline of tribal population in the state as against the slow increment of non-tribal population in the area.

Talking about population, in order to check out the population of Jharkhand in 2018, we need to have a look at the population of the past 5 years. They are as per the following:

1. 2013 – 34.5 Million
2. 2014 – 34.8 Million
3. 2015 – 35.2 Million
4. 2016 – 35.7 Million
5. 2017 – 36.06 Million

Predicting the 2018 population of Jharkhand is not easy but we can get the idea after analysing the population from the year 2013 – 17. As we have seen that every year the population increases by approximate 0.312 Million people. Hence, the population of Jharkhand in 2018 is forecast to be 36.06 Million + 0.312 Million = 36.372 Million. So, the population of Jharkhand in the year 2018 as per estimated data is 36.372 Million.

Jharkhand Population 2018 –36.372 Million. (estimated)..

Demography Of Jharkhand

It has a population of 32.96 million as indicated by the 2011 insights, involving 16.93 Million males and 16.03 million females. The sex proportion of Bihar is 947 females to 1000 males. The population includes 28% tribal social orders, 12% Scheduled Castes and around 60% others. As per 2011 Census of India, Hinduism is the main religion in the state with 67.8% and followed by Islam (14.5%), Christianity (4.1%). Different religions constitute 12.3% of the population, which is basically Sarnaism.

Population Density And Growth Of Jharkhand

The population density of the state is 414 persons per square kilometer. It changes from as low as 148 for every square kilometer in Gumla district to 1167 for every square kilometer in Dhanbad area.

Amid a time when there is a 22.4% growth in the total population, the number of occupants of scheduled tribe has declined by 0.1%. The Primary Census 2011 demonstrated that the total populace in Bihar as on March 1, 2011, was 3,29,88,134. In out and out number, the aggregate population grew in the year 2011, when compared differently in relation to 2001.

Facts About Jharkhand:

1. Cold Weather Season occurs from the long stretch of November to February while Summer Season occurs from March to mid-June.
2. Jharkhand has its air terminals in Ranchi and Jamshedpur. In this manner it is all around connected with aviation routes. It is furthermore connected with Roadways and Railways.
3. The past province of Bihar was parceled into two distinct states of Bihar and Jharkhand.
4. The word Jharkhand suggests The Land of Forests. In regional tongue the significance of Jhar is Gold. In like manner, it can be said that the importance of Jharkhand is a Piece of Gold.
5. Ranchi is the Capital of Jharkhand and it is generally called the modern city.

JHARKHAND DISTRICT WISE POPULATION CENSUS OF 2001

Provisional Population Totals: Jharkhand

The population of the newly created Jharkhand State as at 0:00 hours of 1st March 2001 stood at 26,909,428, as per the provisional results of the Census of India 2001. The population of the State has grown by 23.19% during 1991-2001, which is slightly higher than the country's growth rate of 21.34%. The sex ratio (*i.e.*, the number of females per thousand males) has shown an upward trend. This has gone up from 922 in 1991 to 941 in 2001. Total literacy in the State too has shown significant improvement. This has risen to 54.13% from 41.39% in 1991 Census.

Population:

Persons	:	26,909,428
Males	:	13,861,277
Females	:	13,048,151
Sex Ratio	:	941

Decadal Growth 1991 - 2001:

Persons	:	(+) 23.19 %
Males	:	(+) 21.98 %
Females	:	(+) 24.50 %

Population (0 - 6 years):

Persons	:	4,796,188
Males	:	2,440,025
Females	:	2,356,163
Sex Ratio (0 - 6 years)	:	966

Percentage of Population (0-6) to Total Population:

Persons	:	17.82 %
Males	:	17.60 %
Females	:	18.06 %

Number of Literates:

Persons	:	11,970,177
Males	:	7,759,966
Females	:	4,291,211

Percentage of Literates to Total Population:

Persons	:	54.13 %
Males	:	67.94 %
Females	:	39.38 %

TRIBAL POPULATION PROFILE IN JHARKHAND STATE

Tribals in the State: There are 30 tribes and sub tribes in the Jharkhand region. The major tribes being Santhals, Oraons, Mundas, Kharias, Hos, Cheros, Kherwars, Korwas, Bihores etc. Major dialects in the State are Santhali, Kurukh, Mundari, Kharia, Ho, Sadri, Chotanagpuri etc.

Tribes	*Population*	*% in Tribal Population*	*Literacy within Tribe*
Asur	7783	0.13	10.62
Baiga	3553	0.06	4.22
Banjara	412	lowest	12.38
Bathaudi	1595	0.03	16.93
Bedia	60445	1.04	10.82
Bhumij	136110	2.35	16.45
Binjhia	10009	0.17	14.52
Birhor	4057	0.07	5.74
Birjia	4057	0.07	10.50
Chero	52210	0.09	17.30
Chick Baraik	40339	0.69	20.17
Gond	96574	1.66	20.00
Gorait	5206	0.09	16.61
Ho	536524	9.23	17.71
Karmali	38652	0.66	13.30
Kharia	141771	2.44	24.86
Kharwar	222758	3.83	17.22
Khond	1263	0.02	15.99
Kisan	23420	0.40	13.41
Kora	33951	0.58	9.28
Korba	21940	0.38	6.14
Lohar	169090	2.91	12.71
Mahli	91868	1.59	12.74
Mal Paharia	79322	1.37	7.58
Munda	845887	14.56	22.16

Contd...

Oraon	1048064	18.05	23.28
Parhaiya	24012	0.41	15.30
Santhal	2060732	35.47	12.55
Sauria Paharia	30269	0.68	6.87
Savar	3014	0.05	9.55
Unspecified	6660	0.1	3.94
TOTAL	5810867	100.00	16.99

Abstract Viewer: Growth and Distribution of Tribal Population in Jharkhand 1961-2001: A Census Analysis

The trend of tribal concentration in the state of Jharkhand (India) shows that over time, their share in the state's population is declining, indicating that the tribal population is growing at a slower rate than that of non-tribals. Growth of the tribes, an economically backward social group, indicates their well-being. A distribution of persons having tribal languages as mother tongue gives an indication of tribal migration between Jharkhand and outside areas. Using data on age distribution, we can make rough estimates of vital rates using indirect methods of estimation.

In view of the distortions in the age distribution due to errors of age reporting, three estimates of vital rates are obtained using three methods: Differencing, Stable Population Analysis C(35), and Rele's Revised Method. We conclude that the birth rate, did not change much, but that the death rate has increased, resulting in a reduction in population growth.

GROWTH AND DISTRIBUTION OF TRIBAL

Population in Jharkhand 1961-2001: A Census Analysis

Indigenous people of Jharkhand are the Tribals. Jharkhand is the fifth state of tribal concentration in India. The trend of tribal concentration in the state shows that over time, their share in the state's population is declining and indicates that the tribal population is growing at a slower rate than non-Tribals.

Growth of the Scheduled tribes an economically backward social group, could very well serve as one of the indicators of their well being. Low growth rate, in absence of inter-state migration, may be result of low birth rate and still lower death rate or it may be result of high birth rate and slightly lower death rate. So low growth rate reflect advanced stage of demographic transition or a case of population check as suggested by Malthus.

The growth rate of non-tribals in Jharkhand is more than national growth rate of total population and closed to national tribal growth rate. However, total population growth rate in Jharkhand is less than national growth rate in the entire time period. This suggests that slow growth of tribals in Jharkhand keeps the state growth rate at lower scale.

Among 18 districts of the State, there were 5 tribal districts in 1961 having tribal population more than 50 percent. In 1991 there were only 3 tribal districts. There was not a single district witnessed steady growth in tribal share in each successive census. Tribe wise distribution shows that Santal is the largest tribe constituting about 35% of tribal population of state and other major tribes having population more than 5 lakh are Ho, Munda and Oraon. The Asur, the Birjia, the Korwa, the Mal Paharia, the Sauria Paharia and the Savar are primitive tribes and each contributes around 1 percent or less.

During the decades the population of some tribes (out of 30 tribes) has increased at a very high rate and on the other hand the population of some of the tribes has decreased. These extreme cases are mostly observed among the tribes, which are in small number. The causes for the extreme cases are not explainable through the components of population growth except the internal movements.

Census does not provide information on migration for tribals separately. Another source of information of internal migration is language table. This table provides information of the speakers of the tribal languages as mother tongue. It can be inferred that during the period there was no large-scale movements of tribals between Jharkhand and outside. Thus we can say that the growth of tribal population was due to natural increase only.

From the available data of Tribals, though it is difficult to estimate the levels of birth and death rates, it is possible to have some rough estimates using indirect methods of estimation based on age distribution. In view of the distortions in the census age distribution due to errors of age reporting, it is felt that no single method may prove effective. Hence three estimates of vital rates are obtained using three different methods and are indicative of broad trends rather than actual levels. The three methods considered are Differencing Method, Stable Population Analysis C (35) and Rele's Revised Method.

It is assumed that during each decade the age distribution of tribal population was quasi-stable and stable population method can be used and female birth rate can be obtained and which is then converted into birth rate for total tribal population. Death rate can be obtained from growth rate.

The difference between the population in one census and the population aged 10 years and above in next census is approximately equal to deaths of persons aged 5 years and above. These deaths after multiplying by raising factor will provide death rate. In this method we first arrived at death rate *i.e.* independently from birth rate, which is then converted to Birthrate.

Another method for estimating Birth rate is Rele's method, which does not assume the population to be stable, quasi-stable or closed to migration and hence can be used for estimating fertility levels and trends for sub-national population. Using child women ratios the estimate of GRR and Intrinsic Birth rate is obtained which is then converted to CBR.

Conclusions: The census data show that the tribal population in the state is increasing but their share in the total population is declining. The age structure of tribal population is "young". The rising death rate is the reason for reduction in population growth rate.

Real reason for raising death rate appears to be lack of nutrition and ill health caused by extreme poverty. Spread of industrial and mining waste reduces a land production leads to malnutrition and safe drinking water is not available. Due to malnutrition, incidence of morbidity increases and resistance to infection decreases.

Every village has patients suffering from Malaria and Tuberculosis. Malarial death and morbidity were found to be on rise. Clustered housing pattern in tribal villages also increases the risk of spreading diseases. Any development in tribal land should provide them jobs to buy food otherwise it could be curse for them.

DEMOGRAPHICS

According to the 2011 Indian Census, Jharkhand has a population of 32.96 million, consisting of 16.93 million males and 16.03 million females. The sex ratio is 947 females to 1000 males. The literacy rate of the state was 67.63% with Ranchi district being most educated at 77.13% compared to rural Pakur district being least at 50.17%.

RELIGION

Sun Temple at Ranchi; Hinduism is the largest religion in the state

Religion in Jharkhand (2011)

Hinduism (67.8%)

Islam (14.5%)

Sarnaism (12.8%)

Christianity (4.3%)

Not stated (0.6%)

As per the 2011 census, Hinduism is the majority religion in the state at 67.8%, followed by Islam at 14.5% and Christianity at 4.3%. Other religions, primarily Sarnaism, constitute 12.8% of the population.

CHRISTIANITY IN JHARKHAND

Outer view of Roman Catholic Archdiocese, Ranchi.

Christians are an ethno-religious community residing in the Indian state of Jharkhand. As per 2011 Census of India, 4.3% of people in Jharkhand are Christians. Christians are majority in Simdega district of Jharkhand.

History

Christianity is a minority religion in Jharkhand, a state of India. Most people in Jharkhand are follower of Sarnaism & Hindus. Jharkhand is known for tribals such as Munda, Santhal, Oraon, Kharia people, & Gond. A Roman Catholic Archdiocese of Ranchi exists. St. Mary's Cathedral in Ranchi has been a cathedral since 1909. The Church of North India has a Diocese of Chota Nagpur with a seat at Ranchi. The Church of North India has a St. Paul's Cathedral in Ranchi. Gossner Theological College is in Jharkhand. Many Munda & Kharia are Christians. The then pope visited Ranchi in 1986. The Gossner Evangelical Lutheran Church in Chotanagpur and Assam has its seat in Ranchi. Dhanbad has Oriental Orthodox Churches. Christian missionaries arrived in today's Jharkhand in 1845.

Pre-migration era

By the year 1765 Britishers were successful in their military mobilization to bring Santhal Pargana under British rule. After this conquest the British colonial planters in India as indentured tribal people of the Chota Nagpur Plateau region into Northeast India about 150 years ago for the purpose of being employed in the tea gardens industry as workers and came to be known as Tea tribes.

These tribals were influenced by the Christian missionaries who came along with the British. These Christian missionaries worked for the improvement standard of living and providing education to the children of the tribals by offering money & materials to poor hindu people. Nearly 15 decades later missionaries from Germany left started their voyage to India in 1844 and reached Kolkata (formerly Calcutta) in 1845. These missionaries were initially heading for Mergui in Myanmar (formerly Burma) in view of preaching the Christian faith among the Karen people or in the areas located in the footsteps of the Himalayas. However, on meeting some people from Ranchi, they changed their plan and headed for Chhotanagpur and its main town, Ranchi. They reached Ranchi on 2 November 1845 and camped on, what is now known as, the 'Bethesda Ground' in Ranchi.

Post-migration era

After India got independent the missionaries who remained in post Independence worked for the improvement standard of living and providing education to the children of the tribals. Evidently many of the tribals emerged as sportsman especially in the game of hockey and football. Even the present Prime Minister of India Jawaharlal Nehru in his Discovery of India acknowledges the contribution of the early missionaries for development of tribals dialect stating that

"even laboured at the dialects of the primitive hill and forest tribes. . . .

Culture

Jharkhandi tribal Christian culture retains that of tribal culture in areas such as dress and cuisine. Many Jharkhandi tribal Christians maintain the tribal customs of decoration of bridesand grooms with turmeric.

RELIGION IN JHARKHAND

Hinduism, Islam, Sarna, Christianity, Sikhism are the different religions of Jharkhand. More than 60 percent of the people follow Hinduism. Islam and the animistic Sarna religion each constitute 13 percent of the population. Around four percent of the people follow Christianity. Less than one percent of the population follows Jainism, Buddhism and Sikhism.

The tribal people of Jharkhand follow the animistic Sarna religion. Followers of this religion believe that spirits do exist and they live around us. The Hindus of the state have a different opinion about this religion; they believe that Sarna is a branch of Hinduism.

9

Art, Architecture, Fair and Festivals

TRIBAL ARTWORK

Chhou Mask: Chhou is a type of tribal dance done with colourful masks. The mask made of paper mache in Singhbhum district of Jharkhand. Paper mache' of Saraikela and Charinda are famous for Chhou dance. Some times it appears similar to the masks used in kerla in Kathakali.

Tribal Woodwork: Jharkand is full of good quality saal forest and hence wooden artwork in the should of Tribals of Jharkhand. The wood is used for cooking, housing, farming, fishing etc. The tribal artists of some villages have explored their creativity in art, like beautifully decorative door panels, toys, boxes, and other household articles.

Tribal Bamboo Artwork: The bamboo found in this area are different from bamboos of Southeast Asia. There is tourist place Netarhat in jahrkhand which means a Bazaar of Bamboo. These bamboos are thin in shape and strong and flexible. The tribal people use bamboo for making baskets, hunting & fishing equipments. Specially the bamboo made fishing cage is very attractive.

Triabl Pottery: Tribal pottery is a part of tribals but still no specific working style observed.

Tribal Jewelery: The triabl people particularily like jewelery. They use metallic ornaments made of Gold, Silver, brass, copper for their earrings, nose ring, bracelets, bangles etc.

Godna: Tribals use ornaments a lots but the spiritual concept of ornament is very different. They believe that all ornaments are human made and are mortal. Therefore they invented tattoos as permanent ornament. Majority of tribal woman have tattoos called Godna, on their bodies. However, tribal man also use Godna. They believe that Godna are the only ornament which goes with them after death also.

Tribal Weapons: Bow and arrow is the symbolic weapon of the tribals of this area. Apart from this they use iron made Axes and Doulies and Ghana (Big hammer).

Tribal Metalwork: Most of the metal works are done for agricultural purpose, hunting and weapons. There are specific communities like Lohar, Malhar and Thentri have expertise in metal work.

ART AND CULTURE

Arts & Culture is integral part of Santal society. It reserves vast & rich cultural heritage. Infact Santals are most remembered by their arts and culture. Here we will give some links towards by some of the scholarly works and also some description of it.

First Santali Feature Film. It is land mark for santals. Chandu Lekhon the first full length Santali feature film released last December, 2001. Lakhan Murmu, a famous Santali Jatra artist Cast the lead role as well co-producer. The first of its kind in India. Santali, is the tribal language spoken in Jharkhand, Midnapore, Bardhaman, Orissa, & Purulia would attract the tribals towards cinema. The man behind such noble thought is Jogin Dey the executive producer of the Santali feature film. This film directed by Radha Rani famous Ajit Banerjee; music will be composed by Bappa Chatterjee, new face and Singrai (tribal musician). The playback singers are Tarun Hembram and Shefali Hembram. The script is written in Santali alphabets called Olchiki Script.

SANTHAL MUSICAL INSTRUMENTS

Tirio: The instrument most favoured by Santals, is bamboo flute with seven holes. It is viewed as a symbols of love and seduction.

Dhodro Banam is a bowed instrument carved out of a single log of wood of a tree which according to Santal story, grew out of the flesh of a human being. It consits of a belly (lac) covered with an animal skin on which rests the bridge(sadam, lit, horse), an open chest (korom), a short neck (hotok) and a head (bohok) which is often beautifully carved in the shape of a human head, a couple or whole groups of humans or of animals. If the is a head, the tuning peg is inserted in the ear (lutur), and the gut string comes out the mouth.

Phet Banam is a fretless stringed instrument with three or four strings. The waisted belly is completely covered by animal skin.

Tumdak, is also known as madol, is a two faced drum with a body brunt clay. Both heads the left one broader than the right are covered by bullock hide and are beaten by the left and right hand.

Tamak is a bowl shaped kettle drum. Its body is made of thin metal sheets, covered by bullock hide and beaten by a pair of sticks.

Junko is an onomatopoeic description of sounds of the ankle bells, which are cast in metal in the shape of buds and tied to the feet of dancers from where they produce rhythmical sounds.

Singa is a S-shaped wind instrument played in pairs in weddings. Made of brass of copper, it is usually constructed in the three pierces with mouthpiece at the blowing end and a conic opening at the other.

The tribal art of India is widely neglected in Europe and America. Its meaning is largely unknown and it is generally overshadowed by Classical Indian art. European artists at the beginning of the century made us aware of the arts of Africa and Oceania, and perhaps now we should learn to appreciate the formal language of Indian tribal art as well.

The independent culture of the Adivasi, the tribal inhabitants of India who are not a part of the Hindu caste system in so far as it still exists today, has not yet been thoroughly researched. There is no extensive literature about the Adivasi as exists, for example, for many African cultures. Elsy Leuzinger's Propylaen Kunstgeschichte (1978) reproduces 147 pages of African artifacts, but devotes only 10 pages to Indian tribal art. One of these illustrations depicts a Santal stringed instrument. This object, referred to as a dhodro banam (literally: hollow instrument) forms the basis for this article.

The Santal are the largest group of the Munda people who live in the Indian states of Bihar, Orissa and West Bengal, and subsist primarily by rice farming. Their language, Santali, belongs to the Austroasiatic linguistic family. The patrilinear clan is their largest social unit, and is connected to other clans through marriage. An important part of social life is music, dance and singing in turn. Dances are linked with the fertility of the harvest, and they are performed separately by men and women before and after the rainy season, and between sowing and harvesting. Today, many Santal have adopted Hinduism or Christianity.

Little research has been done about the art of this Indian tribal group. The musical instruments we are addressing here were removed from their original environment by the commercial trade, so it is difficult to retrieve precise information about them, particularly since they have fallen into disuse and have virtually disappeared due to the strong social and cultural pressure of the dominant Hindu population. Despite these obstacles, we will attempt to clarify the situation utilizing the available literature supplemented with observations about instruments in collections, in order to trace the development and meaning of these instruments.

The dhodro banam belongs to the sarinda family, a type of lute with a partially open body that is covered with skin on the lower part. This instrument is played with a bow in the manner of a violin, but in a vertical position, and is found in Iran, Pakistan, Nepal, India and Central Asia.

From a musical viewpoint, the dhodro banam is a simple instrument. It generally has only one string, and its archaic appearance might lead one to suspect that it is the precursor of the sarinda. Its birthplace, however, seems not to have been India but Central Asia. An instrument played by the shamans of that region has the typical characteristics of the sarinda, although it looks quite different on first sight. This instrument, the kobyz, is slightly bow shaped and has a two-part body that is open on the upper half and covered with skin in the lower half.

The Indian musicologist Onkar Prasad considers the dhodro banam to be a regressive form of the sarinda. Other instruments resembling primitively made sarinda are known to exist, including the sarangi of the Gaine, a Nepalese caste of musicians. The body of this instrument has the typical lateral indentations of the sarinda, but it is not so extremely "wasp-waisted".

The form of the dhodro banam is somewhat different, however. Its body is long and is not vaulted like the sarinda. The open part can be separated from the covered part by a step or by a more or less continuous transition, and not by a lateral waist-like indentation. This elongation is not restricted to the dhodro banam; northern Pakistan has a similar long and strongly bent type of instrument, and Curt Sachs, who published a classification method for musical instruments in 1923 that is still in use today, describes a tid or tad of similar form from Punjab and Rajastan. The distribution of the elongated lute is evidently almost identical to that of the rounded form. Thus, at least two types of this stringed lute exist in the cultural area of India that we are examining here: the elongated form that is rounded or slightly broadened at the open part of its body, (*e.g.* dhodro banam and tid), and the form with a sharply pinched waist between the open and skin-covered sections of the body, generally called a sarinda (or sometimes geychak, sarang, sarangi, sarod, etc.). We have yet to know whether a similar long lute was the widespread precursor of today's Indian sarinda or whether it was developed by different societies according to their needs. It is possible that the tribal and rural population continued to use the type that is more easily manufactured, whereas the Hindu and Muslim societies preferred a more sophisticated version.

The narrower form may have been chosen for technical reasons, since it could be made from thinner trees or large branches without having to cut down bigger trees. This apparent advantage is offset by the drawback that the pith core of the wood generally runs through the instrument. Today, it is sometimes difficult to find the appropriate kind of wood, and many of the more recent pieces are worked in inferior material. The pith core has fallen out of some, rendering them useless.

Two other characteristics of the dhodro banam should be mentioned that are indicative of the special development of this instrument. First, the dhodro banam is played in a different manner than the sarinda, in that it is the inner surface of the stretched fingers that presses the string. Second, the carvings on the top of the dhodro banam face the listener. The figures on the peg box of a sarinda are oriented toward the side. This distinction may seem minor, but it implies an autonomous artistic development.

With the exception of the shared characteristics of the elongated body and the rectangular peg box, the appearance of individual dhodro banam varies greatly. The "shoulders" of the instrument may be cut flat, laterally drawn upward, or rounded. Sometimes extensions of the neck protrude prominently into the open part of the body. Elements forming bridges in various configurations are placed on this part, and sometimes take the form of a human being.

The structural transition from the open to the skin-covered parts of the body is contiguous in some instruments, but in others it is clearly articulated as a step. Even the neck varies greatly.

Sometimes it is square, sometimes fully rounded, and sometimes it is rounded with a vertical edge. In some examples, it is hollowed out from the back and in others from the sides. In rare cases, the neck is formed in four columns. Unfortunately, it is not possible today to make positive assertions as to whether such stylistic characteristics are the expression of the exuberant imaginations of individual carvers, local variants of a common form, or the fashion of a certain period in time.

In his book An Introduction to Indian Music (1977), Vishnudass Shirali reproduces some pencil drawings of Santal, Munda and Ho lutes. However, these illustrations are not very precise in their depiction of specific stylistic elements. Some of the pieces represented come from Verrier Elvin's collection, which may be seen in the National Museum in New Delhi. Elvin, a former missionary and anthropologist, adopted the religion of the Gond tribe and is one of the greatest experts on Indian tribal art to have explored its meaning at an early date. Some instruments collected by him have carved tassel-like elements and inset carved registers of ovals that are not observed in more recent instruments.

Since the instruments originate from both Bihar and Orissa, we can assume this to be an impact of time rather than a local variation. Although only the Munda, Ho and Santal tribes are mentioned by Shirali, some ornaments, robes or items of jewelry point to quite different groups. Skulls, for example, do not occur in the art of the Santal.

Figurative representations crowning stringed instruments are found frequently in India, mainly in the east, and in the

Himalayas. Animals are depicted, primarily birds but also horses and goats, mythical animals and, in some cases, groups of animals and human beings. In eastern India the peacock is a particularly popular motif.

The Santal prefer human figures. Animals generally appear only in juxtaposition with human figures, *e.g.*, while being ridden. The crossbars and finials of the peg boxes of the lutes often bear relief or fully articulated carvings of groups of women dancing in a chain, sometimes depicted in multiple registers. These women, dressed in skirts or sari-like costumes, are portrayed performing a dance dedicated to the fertility of the earth.

Sometimes the accompanying dhol (drum), nagara (kettle-drum), shanai (oboe) or dhodro banam player is depicted. In addition to these rows of dancers, two figures, usually female, often decorate the top of the dhodro banam. These figures can be presented realistically or in a simplified manner, and are sometimes even reduced to two small vertical projections.

On lutes of Christianized Adivasi, these figures are re-interpreted and depict Adam and Eve, represented as a naked man and woman. One dhodro banam depicts a woman carrying a naked man. In the tradition of the Muria of the Bastar tribe, this represents a bride and bridegroom. Scenes from everyday life, such as a father, mother and child, horse and elephant riders, and farmers driving carts are popular.

The elements bearing these scenes are also ornamented with lines, circular rosettes, sun symbols and scrolls. With varying skill, later owners often added further ornamentation such as fish, birds, mammals or human beings. The sun symbol is frequently depicted and derives, according to Kamaladevi Chattopadhyaya, from associations with the sun god Sing Bongo. These symbols also appear on the wrists of Santal children as a protection against harm.

The peg boxes of sarinda are invariably crowned or closed at the upper end. The kobyz players of Central Asia adorn this shield-like terminal panel with an odd number of movable pieces of metal that can be made to rattle while the instrument is being played. In eastern India, birds or other animals rest on the panel, which is either round or triangular. Likewise, on eastern Indian sarinda, one finds board-like extensions decorated with metal hearts, circles or other carvings projecting beyond the peg-box. This board-like finial has great significance for the dhodro banam. In older instruments, this element may be as much as one third of the height of the whole.

In India, parts of stringed instruments are traditionally named after parts of the human body. An 18th-century author speaks of "a head, throat, ears and chest" of the sarangi, an instrument similar to the sarinda, and the musician brings forth the voice of the instrument. The Gaine of Nepal likewise claim that their instrument has a mouth, neck, waist and hips. The four strings are named after the members of the family: father, son, daughter and mother. The Santal describe the closed part of the body as the stomach, the open part as the chest, the neck as the neck, and the peg box as the head, in which is stuck the tuning peg, known as the ear.

There have been many efforts to give the instrument the visual attributes of a human being. The body and peg box are carved with faces, but these are usually unseen by the listener since both the body and the peg box are often open in front and the carvings appear behind. More visible is the head that the famous sarangi player Bundu Khan mounted on top of his instrument so that it looked forward and faced the audience.

The dhodro banam, with its thick peg box that looks like a head itself, is reminiscent of a human figure. This impression is reinforced if the peg box is shaped like a head or if the arms are carved laterally on the body of the instument. Some instruments are rendered as a complete figure. Here the instrument maker puts the open part of the body to the rear, so that the resulting surface may be seen as a torso with jewelry, breasts and arms indicated in relief.

In this configuration, an inset in the form of a carved braid of hair may be added to the opening of the peg box to make the head appear complete.

One dhodro banam even has legs. A somewhat similar instrument, called a huka banam, has an element that might be identified as a huge penis, but it may instead be a technical detail and only a finger board.

Male or female genitals are rarely represented, and even breasts are only suggested. The huka banam is of interest because it is held and played in a position that is upside down in relation to the dhodro banam.

When played, the dhodro banam is held vertically in front of the musician, the neck with the striking hand above and the bow hand below. In the case of the huka banam, which rests on the player's chest, the neck and the striking hand are positioned below, and the bow hand above. The huka banam has no pegs and the single string is tied to the neck. Although they are both conceived in anthropomorphic terms, the dhodro banam and huka banam are morphologically unrelated.

A Santal myth reported by the musicologist Onkar Prasad tells the story of seven brothers who one day killed their only sister in order to eat her. The youngest brother, however, could not eat his portion because he so loved his sister, so he buried it in a white ant-hill.

On this spot there grew a beautiful guloic tree, from which a melodious sound was heard. A passing yugi, who often came to pick flowers, heard this sound and decided to cut a branch from the tree to make the first dhodro banam. Prasad notes that the Santal believe the musical instruments to be a gift from supernatural forces. With the assistance of these instruments, they can communicate with entities from other worlds.

They believe that they are physically related to the dhodro banam and consider the instrument to be a human being. This analogy appears to be rooted in both the instrument's anthropomorphic form and its sound, which is reminiscent of the human voice to the Santal people.

This story demonstrates that the dhodro banam has a layered meaning for its players and their audiences. It is more than a simple tool for producing music and there is a deeper meaning behind the instrument's prestigious appearance than a wish for mere attractiveness.

Verrier Elvin reports that the Santal believe that all beauty created by man is destined to disappear with him, and thus the Santal usually bury or burn their exquisitely decorated instruments. This, however, has not always been the general rule. If one studies older examples of dhodro banam in detail, it can be observed that they have been played by several generations.

The patina from use is often quite fresh, although the rest of the instrument may be completely encrusted. Similarly, the awkward decorations that have been added and the different depths of patination point to the fact that an ancient instrument has been recently used. Apparently these instruments were greatly valued, which accounts for their preservation over generations. In the case of figure, even the movable parts were kept. If the body of a precious instrument was destroyed, a new one was grafted to the head. The dhodro banam is used by beggar yugi who move through the villages of India and are the mythical inventors of this instrument. Some sources indicate that dhodro banam players were semi-professional musicians who were invited from afar for festivities.

The creators of the songs of the Santal remain anonymous. As soon as a new song appeared, it became common property. There was no distinction made between the performers and the composer. Whether the dhodro banam was considered a work of art closely connected with the name of its maker or if the maker remained anonymous is not clear. However, the surviving material leads us to believe that the creators of the instruments designed their own models and developed their own styles.

Dhodro banam makers seem to have created basic models that are to be distinguished from one another only by differences in the richness of ornamentation and minor variations in iconography. The same decorative motif, such as a father with mother and child, was clearly produced by several workshops, as can be deduced from variations in stylistic details and in the forms of the body of the instruments. A dark, hard wood was used in the manufacture of the instruments, possibly that of the guloic tree referenced in the myth of origin.

When research on the tribal cultures of India was begun, their civilization was already declining. So far, little attention has been paid to works of art of this kind, and today few important works of art can be found, since the materials used by these tribal peoples were generally perishable. Among the few remaining objects that evidence their culture, we can appreciate the dhodro banam.

CRAFTS

Masks: The masks made in this state is very different from those made in the neighbouring state of Bihar. The masks are rather primitive and fierce and represent what in India is known as tamasik, a manifestation of the moral elemental passions in which every bodily form as well as facial expression is highly exaggerated.

Wood Work: Jharkhand abounds in forests that have a variety of wood for producing several articles of household use. The wood craftspersons of this region carve various attractive articles like door panels, boxes and windows, wooden spoons etc. for household use.

Bamboo Craft: A very thin, flexible and strong variety of bamboo grows in the Jharkhand area. This bamboo lends itself to multifarious uses. Bamboo baskets, containers, hunting equipments and fishing gears are made using this bamboo.

Folk Painting: The Jharkhand area is famous for a special type of folk painting called the paitkar paintings. This form of painting is one of the earliest forms of tribal paintings in India. These paintings have a scrolling look and depicts life after death. However, due to lack of recognition and promotion, this type of painting is slowly facing extinction.

Toy Making: Toupadana near the capital city of Rnchi makes very unusual wooden toys that are completely abstract. They are just pieces of wood painted to look like human figures with angular lines but no separate limbs. Hands are indicated only by painting lines on the body.

The toys are always in pairs -- man and woman waering different crowns, costumes and ornaments. They are breathlessly stunning and very original as they are different from any other doll.

FAIRS

Kunda Mela in Pratappur : This mela is held at the time of falgun Shivratri and is marked by a big sale of cattle.

Kolhua Mela in Hunterganj : It is an ancient fair held twice in a year during Magh Basant panchami and chait Ramnaumi respectively.There is a beautiful lake and ancient temple of Goddess Kali on the top of the hill. Its origin is not known. It is only a religious fair.

Chatra Mela : This mela is said to have started from 1882 and is principally a cattle fair held during Durga Puja.

Kundri Mela in Chatra : The probable year of its origin is 1930 and is held on Kartik purnima and is principally a cattle fair.

Kolhaiya Mela in Chatra : The probable year of origin is 1925. It is held on Magh Basant panchami and is principally a cattle fair.

Tutilawa Mela in Simaria : The probable year of origin is 1935 and is principally a cattle fair held on Falgun purnima.

Lawalong Mela : The probable year of its origin is 1880. It is held at the time of Aghan purnima and is one of the biggest cattle fair of this district.

Belgada Mela in Simaria: The probable year of its origin is 1920 and this is principally a cattle fair held in Baisakh purnima.

Bhadli Mela in Itkhori : There is an ancient temple of Goddess Kali and lord Shiva. The origin of the mela is not known. It is only religious gathering on Makar Sankaranti.

Sangharo Mela in Chatra: It is held in Sawan Purnima. The origin of this fair is not known.

Barura Sharif : There is a shrine of Data Amir Ali shah at Barura Sharif on the bank of Sat Bahini river in Pratappur It is said that the sufi saint came here in the latter half of the 18th century. The Hindus and the Muslim alike come here to pay respect to the reverend saint at his Mazaar. People suffering from evil spirits come here in large number and get themselves cured.

Rabda Sharif: There is a Mazaar (Shrine) of Data Faham Khyal Shah at Rabda Sharif in Pratappur who was contemporary to Data Amir Ali Shah of Barura Sharif. Here annual fair of the saint is celebrated with pomp and grandeur.

The Graveyard of Jatrahibagh: In Jatrahibagh there is a graveyard. It is said that Muslim soldiers of the 1857 mutiny were buried here. It is also known as Anjan Shahid. During British period annual fair was held, hence it is called Jatrahibagh.

Sangat: In Gudri Bazar Mohalla of Chatra there is a Sangat of Udasi Panth of Sikh doctrine where there is an old script of the Holy Gurugranth Saheb. It is venerated at this place and is kept in high esteem by the Sikhs and the Hindus as well. Thus, Chatra is an emblem of communal harmony where the Hindus, the Muslims and the Sikhs reside in peace and harmony.

BARURA SHARIF

Introduction to Barura Sharif : The traditional history of Jharkhand tells the story of a famous Sufi Saint who came and visited Jharkhand in the latter half of the 18th century. This renowned saint, Data Amir Ali Shah was highly respected by all because of the influence and impact he had on the mass by the virtue of his simplicity, love, humanity, purity and miracles. His shrine is located at the Barura Sharif, on the banks of the river Sat Bahini in Pratappur in Jharkhand. He is respected and all people, irrespective of caste, creed and religion, just the way he served humanity without looking into their caste, creed or religion. The shrine at Barura Sharif is located only 12 kilometers from Pratappur and presents a quiet and picturesque sight.

Description of Barura Sharif : The shrine at Barura Sharif was constructed at a height of about 10 feet from the bank of the river. To reach the holy site of Barura Sharif, one has to cross a seasonal stream that passes through this shrine. Locally these small rivers or streams are called 'Saat Bahini' or the seven sisters. The annual fair of the Barura Sharif is held here with a lot of ceremony and gaiety. People from all over, irrespective of what religion they belong to come to pay their homage to the saint, a man highly respected by both Hindus and Muslims. There are hundreds of devotees who come to his Mazaar. All people who suffer from evil spirits also come to the Barura Sharif to cure themselves.

Time for Celebrating Barura Sharif : The Barura Sharif Fair in Jharkhand is held on the eve of Chaitra Navami, which starts from the 1st of the month of Chaitra and lasts till the 10th of the month. The festival ends with the Fatiha Khwani(which is the holy recital of the Quran) on the 10th day of Chaitra.

BHADLI MELA

The people in Jharkhand need a reason to celebrate life. This is evident from the number of fairs and festivals that are held in different state premises throughout the year. Apart from the very popular cattle fairs in Jharkhand, there are also a number of religious fairs and festivals that take place in Jharkhand. People from all over the state and from neighbouring states come together and gather at the venue to observe the occasion and enjoy the celebrations of the fair. The Bhadli fair in Jharkhand is a religious fair which dates back to ancient times.

The Bhadli Fair in Jharkhand takes place in a place called Itkhori. There is an ancient temple belonging to Goddess Kali and Lord Shiva. It is on the day of Maker Sankranti that the Bhadli fair takes place. On the day of the fair, people from all over gather together for celebrations. The origin of such a religious gathering is still not known.

Other than the cattle fairs in Jharkhand like the Chatra fair, the Kundri Mela, the Kolhaiya Mela and others, there are other fairs and festivals held for different reasons.

These include along with Bhadli fair, fairs and festival such as the Graveyard of Jatrahibagh, the Sangat, the Sangharo Mela, the Rabda Sharif and the Barura Sharif. The Sangharo mela take place in Chatra on the day of Sawan Purnima and like many other fairs, its origin is also not known. Both Rabda Sharif and the Barura Sharif are shrines of saints and there are fairs of the saints celebrated with a lot of zeal and passion every year.

KOLHAIYA MELA

The state of Jharkhand has earned quite a name as the venue for an endless number of fairs and festivals. These fairs in Jharkhand held with much pomp and splendour give the people of Jharkhand a refreshing break from time to time. There are a number of cattle fairs in Jharkhand, of which the Kolhayia Mela in Chatra is a reputed name.

Though principally a cattle fair in Chatra, like the Kundri Mela, the Kolhaiya mela too is held with a great zeal. It takes place on the day of Magh Basant Panchami. The Kolhaiya Mela, like other cattle fairs in Jharkhand originated much earlier, around the year 1925.

Chatra Mela is the principal cattle fair in Jharkhand. The Kolhaiya Mela along with the Kundri mela are the other cattle fairs in Chatra. There are also the Tutilawa Mela and the Belgada mela in Simaria, and Lawalong mela which comprise of the rest of the cattle fairs her in Jharkhand.

KUNDA MELA IN PRATAPPUR

Introduction to Kunda Mela in Pratappur: There is always some fair or festival happening in some part of Jharkhand that keeps the people living here busy all year through.. Kunda Mela in Pratappur, Jharkhand is mainly a fair for cattle trade. It takes place in the Chatra District of Jharkhand. It is one of the largest and wide scale fairs that is held in Jharkhand. Participants, buyers and sellers of cattle trek through long distances of dusty roads with their cattle to take part in the Kunda Mela in Jharkhand. Some people also colour and dress up their cattle to make them look unique while coming to the Kunda Mela.

Description of Kunda Mela in Pratappur: It is during the occasion of Shivratri that the Kunda Mela takes place. It is attended by people from all over the states well as the neighbouring states, such as West Bengal and Chatisgarh. The Kunda Mela involves buying and selling of cattle, which is one of the chief sources of livelihood for the people there. This makes the Kunda Mela one of the most significant fairs in Jharkhand. The Kunda Mela is enjoyed not only by the buyers and sellers of cattle, but also other people of Jharkhand who flock to experience the ambience which is unique to an Indian fair - delicious aromas, excited din, and festive colours!

Time for Celebrating Kunda Mela in Pratappur : It is around the time of Falguni Shivratri that the Kunda Mela in Pratappur is held.

LAWALONG MELA

Jharkhand is noted for its fairs and festivals and there is always some fair or festival happening in the state, keeping the people in a festive mood throughout the year. There are a number of fairs held in memory of some saint or a pir. Jharkhand is also well known for the number of cattle fairs that take place here. People from near and far travel through the dusty roads to be a part of this festive extravaganza. One such cattle fair in Jharkhand is the Lawalong Mela.

The Lawalong Mela in Jharkhand is an ancient fair that started from about the year 1880. Since then till now, the Lawalong Mela has taken place almost every year. It has emerged as the biggest and one of the most popular of the cattle fairs in Jharkhand. The Lawalong Fair takes place on the day of the Aghan Purnima.

Other cattle fairs in the district of Jharkhand are also petty well known and visited by a number of people from all over the state. These fairs are the Chatra mela, the Kundra Mela and the Kolhaiya Mela in Chatra, the Tutilawa fair and the Belgada mela of Simaria.

SANGAT

The word 'Sangat' is the Punjabi version of the word 'Sangti' which means company. It can also be referred to as some form of fellowship or association. In the vocabulary of the Sikhs, the word 'Sangat' holds a special significance. It means a group of men, women or children who come together for a religious meet, especially in the company of the Guru Granth Sahib. The Guru Granth Sahib is the holy book of the Sikhs, a collection of devotional poems, hymn and songs that speaks of morality, humanity of the soul and salvation with God. The Sangat in Jharkhand is thus a significant religious gathering of the Sikhs.

Common use of the word Sangat' now refers to any gathering of the Sikhs, either at a Gurudwara, or a private residence, in the presence of the Guru Granth sahib, for the purpose of a religious prayer, social ceremony or instruction. It is in the Gudri Bazaar district or Mohalla of Chatra in Jharkhand that the Sangat of Udasi Panth of Sikh doctrine takes place.

The Udasis was an ascetic group who claimed to be the descendents of Baba Shri Chand JI, one of the two sons of Guru Nanak and the path they followed; very different from the Khalsa was the Udasi Panth. This place holds special significance because of the fact that there is an ancient script of the Guru Granth Sahib here. This doctrine is respected and venerated and kept in high esteem here by both the Hindus and the Muslims in Jharkhand.

TUTILAWA MELA

Jharkhand celebrates their rich culture and livelihood with a number of fairs and festivals. So it is at every fortnight that there is some fair or festival happening in some part of the state. People from all over the state as well as from the neighbouring states come to be a part of the grand celebrations and enjoy the revelry of a fair. Cattle fairs in Jharkhand are some of the most popular of the fairs and festivals in Jharkhand. It is not only for the buying and selling of cattle which makes them a grand affair, but also the other enjoyments of a fair such as the races, swinging, acrobatics and wrestling bouts. One such a fair is the Tutilawa Mela in Jharkhand.

It is around the year 1935 that the Tutilawa fair originated in Jharkhand. This is a fair where principally there is buying and selling of cattle. Villagers from far off comes with their cattle to the Tutilawa fair. It is on the auspicious day of Falgun Purnima that the Tutilawa fair takes place.

Other cattle fairs worth mentioning in Jharkhand are the Chatra Mela, The Kundri mela, The Kolhaiya mela, Lawalong Mela and Belgada mela. All these fairs in Jharkhand are held on different days and all are principally cattle fairs. But there are other activities that makes the fair much more jovial and interesting and give all enough reasons to celebrate.

BELGADA MELA

Cattle fairs in Jharkhand are of an immense popularity. People from near and far, from the state as well as from the neighbouring states come to these fairs to buy or sell their cattle. The cattle fairs give everyone a reason to rejoice and take a respite from the mundane day to day living. These fairs also help them in their business. Of the cattle fairs in Jharkhand, one which is pretty well known is the Belgada Mela.

The Belgada mela takes place on the day of Baisakhi Purnima. Probably the year in which the Belgada Fair originated was 1880.

This is also essentially cattle fair though there are other festivities of a fair that can be enjoyed by all during this time. The other cattle fairs in Jharkhand are the Chatra mela which is held during the Durga Puja and two other fairs that take place in Chatra as well.

These are the Kundri Mela which is held on Kartik Purnima and the Kolhaiya Mela held on the day of Magh Panchami. Other cattle fairs in Jharkhand are the Titulawa Mela that is held on Falgun Purnima and the Lawalong Mela, held on the day of the Aghan Purnima.

CHATRA MELA

Anyone who cherishes a rich culture would love to visit Jharkhand because of its fondness for fairs and festivals. There is always some kind of a celebration that prevails in the air. The people express their vivacity in the form of fairs and festivals in Jharkhand. There are a number of cattle fairs that take place in Jharkhand. One such popular cattle fair is the Kundri Mela in Jharkhand.

The Kundri Mela in Chatra is the principal cattle fair in Jharkhand. It was as early as 1882 that this cattle fair started in Jharkhand and since then it has been held every year in the state. The Kundri Fair takes place during the month of September/October, around the time of the Durga Puja.

Some other cattle fairs held in Jharkhand other than the Kundri Mela are the Chatra mela, Kolhaiya Mela, Tutilawa Mela, Lawalong Mela and the Belgada Mela..

The Kundri Mela in all probability started much later than the Chatra Fair, in the year 1930 while the Kolhaiya Mela began in the year 1925 and the Belgada Mela about 5 years before. It was around the same time span, in the year 1935 that the Tutilawa Mela began to be held in Jharkhand. The Lawalong Fair comparatively dates back to an earlier time, around the year 1880. All of these are principally cattle fairs in Jharkhand which contributes to a great extent in keeping the festive spirit in the air.

KOLHUA MELA IN HUNTERGANJ

Introduction to Kolhua Mela: Jharkhand is well noted for the number of fairs that are held in its premises. All these fairs have active participation from the enthusiastic people, which makes Jharkhand a cheerful and a vivacious state in India. The Kolhua Mela is one such fair in Jharkhand that takes place twice a year in a place called Hunterganj. Hunterganj is at a distance of about 190 kilometers, north of the Kolhua Hill in the Chatra district of Jharkhand.The Kolhua Mela takes place on the top of the Kolhua Hills where an ancient Kali Temple is located. The Kolhua Hills lie about 6 miles south east of Hunterganj.

Description of Kolhua Mela: The Kolhua Mela in Hunterganj is a very ancient fair of Jharkhand. This Mela takes place on the top of the Kolhua Hill. There is an ancient temple of Goddess Kali on top of the hill. The origin of the temple is not known yet by the historians. The temple is also called the temple of the 'Kuleshwari Devi'. There is also a water tank on the top. The Kolhua Mela is a religious fair in Jharkhand. On this day a number of pilgrims and devotees flock to the top of the hill to worship the Goddess. To attend the Kolhua Mela in Jharkhand, one has to trek to the top of the hill. It is not an easy trek as the roads are steep and there are no rest houses. But the place is serene and beautiful and one is most likely to forget of the fatigue once he/she reaches the top of the Kolhua Hill and looks around.

Time for Celebrating Kolhua Mela: The Kolhua Mela in Jharkhand is celebrated twice every year. The times for celebrating the Kolhua Mela are during Magh Vasanth Panchami and Ram Navami.

KUNDRI MELA

There is always some kind of a fair or a festival that happens in Jharkhand keeping the people busy and occupied. It is not that anyone complains since the fun loving and cheerful people of Jharkhand love them. From the fairs and festivals in Jharkhand, the most prevalent fairs are the cattle fairs in Jharkhand. One such cattle fair is the Kundri Mela in Jharkhand.

The Kundri Fair or the Kundri Mela in Jharkhand principally deals with the buying and selling of cattle. This cattle fair is held on the day of the Kartik Purnima. It is said that the Kundri Mela originated in the year 1930, way before India became independent and much before Jharkhand became a separate state.

There are also a number of other cattle fairs in Jharkhand. There is the Chatra Mela, held during the time of the Durga Puja. Other Mela in Chatra other than the Kundri mela is the Kolhaiya Mela, held during the time of Magh Basant Panchami. Other cattle fairs are the Tutilawa Mela that takes place on the day of Falgun Purnima, the Lawalong Mela which takes place on the day of the Aghan Purnima and the Belgada Mela in Baisakhi Purnima.

RABDA SHARIF

There is no end to the time for merriment in Jharkhand, which is always wrapped up in some kind of revelry or the other, in the form of fairs and festivals. In Jharkhand, fairs are also held to pay homage to Sufi saints who visited Jharkhand long time back. The fairs are held around their mazaar, such as the Rabda Sharif or the Barura Sharif, to pay respect to them and the contribution they had over humanity as a whole.

Data Faham Khyal Shah was a contemporary to Data Amir Ali Shah who is a greatly revered and respected Sufi saint, popular with people of all religions, be it the Hindus or the Muslims. The mazaar or the shrine of Data Faham Khyal Shah is situated at Rabda Sharif in Pratappur.

There is an annual fair that is held to pay homage to the saint. This fair at Rabda Sharif is celebrated with a lot of enthusiasm and passion by all the devotees and there is a wide participation of the people who flock here from in and around the state.

Apart from the Rabda Sharif, the other very renowned and visited mazaar is at the Barura Sharif that of the famed Sufi saint Data Amir Ali Shah. He had a powerful influence over all humanity by the virtue of his views on religion, love, respect and because of his impartiality towards any particular creed or caste, he is still respected by all, both Hindus and Muslims. The fair at the Barura Sharif takes place on a wider scale than Rabda Sharif which nevertheless is a significant fair in Jharkhand.

FAIRS AND FESTIVALS IN JHARKHAND

Situated on the eastern side of the Vindhya hills and at the northern fringes of the Deccan is the beautiful state of Jharkhand. Blessed by nature and known for its rich and diverse culture, Jharkhand is visited by large number of tourists every year. Jharkhand is home to large number of fairs and festivals celebrated throughout the year.

Famous for its rich culture especially the tribal culture, Jharkhand is a home to number of fairs and festivals celebrated all the year round. Besides, the cattle play a very important role in the fairs and festivals of Jharkhand. You will see big cattle fair, which includes sale and purchase of cattle in most of these festivals.

Held at the time of Phalgun Shivratri, Kunda Mela in Pratappur is one of the major festivals of Jharkhand and is marked by the sale of cattle.

Started in 1882, Chatra Mela is another major festival of Jharkhand and is mainly a cattle fair held during Durga Puja.

Besides, Kundri Mela, Kolhaiya Mela, Tutilawa Mela, Lawalong Mela, Belqada Mela, Sangharo Mela etc. are some of the other important fairs and festivals in Jharkhand.

The mesmerizing locale of Jharkhand is endowed with the reputation of being one of those states in the country of India that proudly celebrates an entire caboodle of festivals with unparalleled vigor and incomparable zeal. As a matter of fact, the residents are so jolly, fun-loving and hospitable and the way they celebrate the Jharkhand fairs and festivals, you are in for a huge surprise.

The various cattle fairs that are held inside the premises of the state of Jharkhand form an integral appendage of the Jharkhand fairs and festivals. A good majority of them basically pivot around the exchange of exquisitely ornamented cattle for thick bundles of green stuff. These fairs and festivals of Jharkhand also provide scope for a lot of co-curricular and amusement related activities which rejuvenates and invigorates every soul in sight. These activities that have virtually become the identity of Jharkhand include wrestling bouts where the wrestlers possessing herculean physique put up a brave display of brute strength and amazing maneuver, swimming, acrobatic acts that will completely dazzle you and many more.

The fairs and festivals in Jharkhand include a large number of fairs involving the monetary exchange of cattle. Some of the most prominent are Kunda Mela in Pratappur, Chatra Mela, Lawalong Mela, Sangharo Mela, Tutilawa Mela.

The major and most celebrated festivals at Jharkhand include Holi which is celebrated with a lot of enthusiasm and vigor. Dussehra that marks the magnanimous victory of Prince Ram over the demon of Lanka who had ten heads, Ravana and Ramanavami which is basically the celebration of Prince Ram's birthday.

Holi in Jharkhand

Holi in Jharkhand is one of those legendary festivities that is feted in a truly spectacular and grand way. Holi at Jharkhand is principally celebrated in a grand way in the month of Phalgun according to Hindu calendar which merges with the months of February and March in the English calendar. Dhanbad serves to be the venue that oversees this jovial and invigorating carnival of colors.

The folks at Jharkhand immensely believe the legend of Holika and have kept the tradition of igniting a bonfire alive till now. The people engage themselves in all sorts of activities related with fun and jubilation.

The vigor and enthusiasm with which Holi in Jharkhand is celebrated by the people truly deserves a huge round of applause. They forget all sorts of discriminations regarding cast or creed and merge together to get drenched in the rejoicing spirit of this spectacular carnival.

Dussehra in Jharkhand

Dussehra in Jharkhand is considered to be of high priority as far as these festivals are concerned. As a matter of fact, Dussehra is not only feted across the domain of Jharkhand, but across the entire country of India. This momentous occasion is cordially feted on precisely the tenth day of 'Ashwayuja' or 'Ashwina', which are the names given to the Hindu calendar.

Like the rest of the festivities, Dussehra in Jharkhand also marks the triumph of godliness and truth over the dark and evil forces. Dussehra at Jharkhand simultaneously indicates the conclusion of 'Navratri' that is celebrated over a span of nine days as the name suggests. One aspect of Dussehra of

Jharkhand is that it people from all caste and creed can participate in it.

TRIBAL FESTIVALS

Sarhul: Sarhul is celebrated during spring season and the Shaal trees get new leaves. It is a worship of the village deity who is considered to be the protector of the tribes. People sing and dance a lot when the new leaves appear. The deities are worshipped with shaal flowers. These shaal flowers represents the brotherhood and friendship among villagers and Pahan the priest, distributes shaal flowers to every villager. Then the Prasad is distributed among villagers. The Prasad is a rice made wine called Handia

Karam: This festival is a worship of Karam devta, the god of power, youth and youthfulness. Karam festivals is held on the 11th day of the phases of moon in Bhadra month. The groups of young villagers go to jungle and collect wood, fruits and flowers. These are required during the Puja of Karam God. During this entire period people sing and dance in groups. The entire valley seems to be dancing with the drumbeats. This is one of the rare example of such a vital and vibrant youth festival in Jharkhand's Tribal area.

At the same time, the unmarried young tribal girls celebrate the Jawa festival, which has its own kind of songs and dance. This is held mainly for the expectation of good fertility and better household. The unmarried girls decorate a small basket with germinating seeds. It is believed that the worship for good germination of the grains would increase the fertility. The girls offer green melons to the Karam deity as a symbol of 'son' which reveals the primitive expectation of human being, i.e grains and children. The entire tribal area of Jaharkhand becomes tipsy during this time.

Tusu Parab or Makar: This festival is mostly seen in the area between Bundu, Tamar and Raidih area of Jaharkhand. This belt has a great history during India's independence movement. TUSU is a harvest festival held during the winter in the last day of Poush month. It is also for the unmarried girls. Girls decorate a wooden/ bamboo frame with coloured paper and then gift it to the nearby hilly river. Although there is no documented history available on this festival but it has huge collection of scintillating songs full of life and taste. These songs reflect the simplicity and innocence of tribal people.

Hal Punhya: Hal Punhya is a festival which begins with the fall of winter. The first day of Magh month, known as "Akhain Jatra" or "Hal Punhya", considered as the beginning of ploughing. The farmers, to symbolize this auspicious morning plough two and half circles of their agricultural land this day is also considered as the symbol of good fortune.

Bhagta Parab: This festival comes between the period of spring and summer. Among the tribal people of Jharkhand this festival is best known as the worship of Budha Baba. People fast during the day and carry the bathing Pahan the priest, to the tribal mandir called Sarana Mandir.

The Pahan sometimes called Laya, gets out of the pond, the devotees make a chain, locking their thighs with each other and come forward to offer their bare chest to Laya for walk over. After worship in the evening, devotees take part in dynamic and vigorous Chhau Dance wit lots of gymnastic actions and masks.

The next day is full of primitive sports of bravery. The devotees pierce hooks on skin and get tied at one end of a long horizontal wooden pole, which is hanging on the top of a vertical Shal wood pole. The height goes up to 40 feet. The other end of the pole which is connected with a rope, pulled around the pole by the people and the tied devotee display the breath-taking dance in the sky. This festivals is more popular in the Tamar region of Jharkhand.

Rohin: This festival is perhaps the first festival of Jharkhand. It is a festival of sowing seeds in the field. Farmers starts sowing seeds from this day but there is no dance or song like other tribal festivals but just a few rituals. There are some other festivals like Rajsawala Ambavati and Chitgomha are also celebrated with Rohin.

Bandna: Bandana is one of the most famous festivals celebrated during the black moon of month of Kartik (Kartik Aamavashya). This festival is mainly for the animals. Tribals are very close with animals and pets. In this festival, people wash, clean, paint, decorate feed well and put ornaments to their cows and bulls. The song dedicated for this festival is called Ohira which is an acknowledgement for animal's contribution in their day-to-day life. The belief behind this festival is animals are integral part of life and have souls as human being do. The most exciting day of the bandana week is the last day. Closured Bulls and buffalos are chained to a strong pole and they are attacked with a dry animal Hyde. The angry animals hit the dry skin with its horns and the crowd enjoys. Generally the colour used for decorating animals are natural colours and the is artwork is of folk type.

FESTIVALS IN JHARKHAND

Sarhul is a festival where Shaal tree and leaves play an important role. Sarhul is celebrated during the spring season when the Shaal trees get new leaves. Shaal flowers are brought to saran sthal (the sacred place) and pahan propitiates the Gods. The priest is called Pahan and he distributes shaal flowers to every villager. The shaal flowers represent the brotherhood and friendship among villagers. It is believed that the earth becomes fertile after this festival as such sowing is taken up.

Santhals, the largest community in Jharkhand, celebrates the same festival as the festival of flowers and calls it Baha. Besides sal, mahua flowers are also used as an important item for the rituals. Santhals celebrate Sohrai with grand festivity. It is preceded by Dansi.

Dansi coincides with Durga Puja while Sohrai is celebrated immediately after Diwali or Kali Puja. Dansi is a dance festival, though not an elaborate ritual function. A small ritualistic act is observed before the dance begins at akhara.

Sohrai is known for the care of domestic animals such as cows and buffaloes. Since these animals are significant in an agricultural society, taking proper care and welfare of them form important ritual of Sohrai. It is celebrated immediately after diwali, on the new moon day. In the evening, earthen lamps are lighted. The next day the cattle are washed, vermilion mixed with oil is put on the cattle and they are garlanded. The festivities include such games as bull fights.

Karma is another festival in Jharkhand that has a close link with nature. Karam Devta, the God of Power, youth and youthfulness is worshipped during the festival. The festival is held on the 11th day of the phases of moon in the Bhadra month. Young girls celebrate this festival for the welfare of their brothers. This ritual is known as jawa. This is held mainly in expectation of good fertility and better household. The unmarried girls decorate a small basket with germinating seeds. It is believed that the worship for good germination of the grains would increase the fertility. The girls offer green melons to the Karam deity as a symbol of 'son' which reveals the primitive expectation of human being, i.e. grains and children. On the day of festival, brothers bring branches of karam tree that are placed in the courtyard. These branches, symbolizing Karma god, are worshipped by the sisters. These are ceremoniously immersed in a local pond or river the next day. During this entire period people sing and dance in groups. The entire valley seems to be dancing with the drumbeats. This is one of the rare examples of such a vital and vibrant youth festival in Jharkhand's Tribal area. The entire tribal area of Jharkhand becomes tipsy during this time.

Tusu Parab or Makar: This festival is mostly seen in the area between Bundu, Tamar and Raidih area of Jharkhand. TUSU is a harvest festival held during the winter in the last day of Poush month. It is also for the unmarried girls. Girls decorate a wooden/ bamboo frame with coloured paper and then contribute it to the nearby hilly river.

Hal Punhya: Hal Punhya is a festival which begins with the fall of winter. The first day of Magh month, known as "Akhain Jatra" or "Hal Punhya", considered as the beginning of Ploughing. The farmers, to symbolize this auspicious morning plough two and half circles of their agricultural land this day is also considered as the symbol of good fortune.

Bhagta Parab: This festival comes between the period of spring and summer. Among the tribal people of Jharkhand this festival is best known as the worship of Budha Baba. People fast during the day and carry the bathing Pahan the priest, to the tribal mandir called Sarana Mandir. The Pahan sometimes called Laya, gets out of the pond, the devotees make a chain, locking their thighs with each other and come forward to offer their bare chest to Laya for walk over. After the worship in the evening, devotees take part in dynamic and vigorous Chhau dance with lots of gymnastic actions and masks. The next day is full of primitive sports of bravery. The devotees pierce hooks on skin and get tied at one end of a long horizontal wooden pole, which is hanging on the top of a vertical Shaal wood pole. The height goes up to 40 feet. The other end of the pole which is connected with a rope is pulled around the pole by the people and the tied devotee display the breath-taking dance in the sky. This festival is more popular in the Tamar region of Jharkhand.

Rohin: This festival is perhaps the first festival of Jharkhand in the calendar year. It is a festival of sowing seeds in the field. Farmers start sowing seeds from this day but there is no dance or song like other tribal festivals but just a few rituals. There are some other festivals like Rajsawala Ambavati and Chitgomha which are also celebrated with Rohin.

Bandna: Bandana is one of the most famous festivals celebrated during the black moon month of Kartik (Kartik Aamavashya). This festival is mainly for the animals. Tribals are very close with animals and pets. In this festival, people wash, clean, paint, decorate feed well and put ornaments to their cows and bulls. The song dedicated for this festival is called Ohira which is an acknowledgement for animal's contribution in their day-to-day life.

The belief behind this festival is animals are integral part of life and have souls as human being do. The most exciting day of the bandana week is the last day. Closured Bulls and buffalos are chained to a strong pole and they are attacked with a dry animal Hyde. The angry animals hit the dry skin with itchier horns and the crowd enjoys. Generally the colours used for decorating animals are natural colours and this artwork is of folk type.

10

Education

INTRODUCTION

As per the 2011 census conducted by Government of India the official literacy rate for the state was 67.63% (male: 78.45%; female: 56.21%) with nine districts above the average literacy rate:

- Ranchi: 77.13% (male: 85.53%; female: 68.20%)
- East Singhbhum: 76.13% (male: 84.51%; female: 67.33%)
- Dhanbad: 75.71% (male: 85.68%; Female: 64.70%)
- Ramgarh: 73.92% (male: 83.51%; female: 63.49%)
- Bokaro: 78.48% (male: 84.50%; female: 61.46%)
- Hazaribagh: 70.48% (male: 81.15%; female: 59.25%)
- Saraikela Khasawan: 68.85% (male: 81.01%; female: 56.19%)
- Kodarma: 68.35% (male: 81.25%; female: 54.77%)
- Lohardaga: 68.29% (male: 78.62%; female: 57.86%)
- Deoghar: 66.34% (male: 79.13%; female: 53.39%)

Since the formation of the new state, the Jharkhand Education Project Council (JEPC) has been implementing four projects to spread elementary education: DPEP, SSA, NPEGEL, and KGBV. The state has been moving towards the goal of universal elementary education but the target of 100%

enrolment and retention of children in schools has not yet been attained. Jharkhand has made primary education so accessible that 95% of children of ages 6–11 are enrolled in school, as opposed to 56% in 1993–94; this will likely improve literacy a great deal.

Schools

The medium of instruction in schools is Hindi/English with English/Hindi/Sanskrit/Bengali/Odia as second language. After 10 years of schooling, students can join 2 years of Intermediate course (or +2 courses) in Arts, Science and Commerce.

This is followed by 3 years of degree courses (graduation) or 4 years of Engineering/Agriculture/Medicine degree.

On May 2008, Jharkhand became the first in India to introduce free haircuts for poor students. 40,000 barbers will be employed with a monthly salary of 1000 rupees (25 US dollars) which will cost the state government 40 million rupees (1 million US dollars).

Universities and colleges

- Birsa Agricultural University, Kanke, Ranchi
- Central University of Jharkhand, Brambe, Ranchi
- Jharkhand Rai University, Ranchi
- Kolhan University, Chaibasa
- National University of Study and Research in Law, Ranchi
- Nilamber Pitamber University, Medininagar
- Ranchi University, Ranchi
- Sido Kanhu Murmu University, Dumka
- Vinoba Bhave University, Hazaribagh

Autonomous

- Indian Institute of Information Technology, Ranchi
- Indian Institute of Management Ranchi
- Indian Institute of Technology (Indian School of Mines), Dhanbad

- National Institute of Foundry and Forge Technology (NIFFT), Ranchi
- National University of Study and Research in Law
- National Institute of Technology, Jamshedpur
- St. Xavier's College, Ranchi
- Xavier Institute of Social Service (XISS), Ranchi
- Xavier Labour Relations Institute (XLRI), Jamshedpur

Agriculture

- Indian Institute of Agricultural Biotechnology, Ranchi

Engineering

Birla Institute of Technology, Mesra, Ranchi

- Birla Institute of Technology, Mesra, Ranchi
- Birsa Institute of Technology Sindri, Dhanbad
- Cambridge Institute of Technology, Ranchi
- DAV Institute of Engineering & Technology, Daltonganj

Management

- Institute of Management Studies, Ranchi IMS-RU

Medical colleges

- M.G.M. Medical College, Jamshedpur
- Patliputra Medical College and Hospital (PMCH), Dhanbad
- Rajendra Institute of Medical Sciences (RIMS), Ranchi

Psychiatry

- Central Institute of Psychiatry

PUBLIC HEALTH

Because of its mild climate, Jharkhand, particularly its capital Ranchi, has been like a health resort. As far back as 1918, facilities were set up for treatment of mentally challenged. European Mental Hospital was established along with Indian Mental Hospital. Today they are called Central Institute of Psychiatry and Ranchi Institute of Neuro-psychiatry and Allied Sciences respectively. In certain areas of Jharkhand, poverty and consequent malnutrition have given rise to diseases like tuberculosis (TB). In fact, TB has assumed epidemic proportions in certain areas of the state. For management and treatment of such TB, Itki TB Sanatorium, Ranchi, established in 1928 has been doing exemplary work as a premier institute for clinical and programmatic management of TB. The Itki TB Sanatorium is well equipped and accredited by the Indian government for quality assurance and Culture and Drug Sensitivity Testing for M.TB. It provides free of cost treatment for TB as well as Drug resistant TB. Likewise, in the field of treatment of cancer, Tata Main Hospital, Jamshedpur, is rendering pioneering work. In the same way Bokaro General Hospital equipped with modern facilities for the treatment Cancer and heart related problems with capacity of 1100 beds one of the largest in eastern India.

Although several public and private health facilities are available in the state, overall infrastructure for dispensing health related services require improvements. An exception is the famous Tata Motors Hospital which is an example of an ISO 14001 and 18001 certified hospital with DNB teaching facilities.

Ranchi, the capital, has witnessed a sharp growth in the number of hospitals. Hospitals like Orchid Medical Centre have introduced world class healthcare services to the people of the state. However, in rural areas facilities are still scarce and reliant on foreign aid projects (such as Traditional Healthcare in Datom) for the establishment of clinics

Fluoride in groundwater presents a public health problem in Jharkhand. A recent survey led by the Birla Institute of Technology, Mesra, Ranchi in collaboration with UNICEF in the northwest districts of Palamau and Garhwa found fluoride levels above the drinking WHO drinking water guidelines. Excessive amounts of fluoride in drinking water can lead to dental fluorosis, prevalent bone fractures, and skeletal fluorosis, an irreversible disabling condition. Some work has focused on combating fluorosis through increased calcium intake by consuming local plants. Researchers at Princeton University and the Birla Institute of Technology, Mesra, Ranchi are currently investigating defluoridation options, while performing an epidemiological survey to assess the extent of fluoride linked health problems and the impact of future interventions.

Almost 80% of Jharkhand's people are farmers, although it contains 40% of India's mineral reserves it has some of India's poorest people, in Summer 2009 the state was threatened by drought, with people criticising the government for not providing food aid or assistance.

SPORTS

Cricket, hockey, and football are popular games with the people of Jharkhand. Jharkhand has given some brilliant players like Jaipal Singh, a former Indian hockey captain and Olympian and Manohar Topno, currently playing for the Indian Hockey team. Jaipal Singh was the captain of the hockey team that won the first gold medal for India in the 1928 Summer Olympics in Amsterdam. Mahendra Singh Dhoni who was the captain of Indian cricket team and led the Indian cricket team to ICC Cricket World Cup Glory on 2 April 2011, ending a 28-year wait to repeat the feat achieved by former Indian captain Kapil Dev in 1983 at Lord's, England.

Aerial View of JRD Tata Sports Complex and Keenan Stadium in Jamshedpur

Another rising cricketer from Jharkhand is Varun Aaron, India's fastest bowler and Saurabh Tiwary, left hand hard hitting batsman of India who represented Mumbai Indians from the 2008 Indian Premier League and currently playing for Delhi Daredevils in 2015. He was one of the key batsmen in the Indian team that won the 2008 U/19 Cricket World Cup in Malaysia. Ashunta Lakra, sister of Vimal Lakra is the Indian Hockey Captain currently.And one of the emerging sport personality is Deepika Kumari, a young Indian athlete who competes in the event of Archery. She won gold medal in the 2010 Commonwealth games in the women's individual recurve event.

An International Cricket stadium with an indoor stadium and a practice ground has been constructed. This international stadium has hosted an International Match between India and England on 19 January 2013. Apart from that, this stadium has hosted two IPL 6 matches for KKR and qualifier 2 of IPL 8between CSK and RCB and Celebrity Cricket League Matches for Bhojpuri Dabanggs. A Tennis Academy, which was inaugurated by Sania Mirza and Shoaib Malik, also runs besides the Cricket stadium. Ranchi is among six cities in Hockey India League to be played in January 2013. Ranchi franchise was bought by Patel-Uniexcel Group and the team named Ranchi Rhinos which is now being co-hosted by Mahendra Singh Dhoni and named as Ranchi Rays. Ranchi is also famous for being the hometown of World Cup winning Captain of Indian Cricket team, Mahendra Singh Dhoni. India's ace archer Deepika Kumari, gold medal winner of Commonwealth Games 2010 and current world no.1 rank holder, also hails from Ranchi.

LIST OF INSTITUTIONS OF HIGHER EDUCATION IN JHARKHAND

Autonomous institutions

- Amity University, Ranchi, Jharkhand
- Jharkhand Rai University, Ranchi, Jharkhand

- ICFAI University, Ranchi, Jharkhand
- Sarala Birla University, Ranchi, Jharkhand
- Birsa Institute of Technology, Sindri, Dhanbad
- Indian Institute of Management, Ranchi (IIM Ranchi)
- Indian Institute of Technology (Indian School of Mines), Dhanbad
- Indian Institute of Information Technology, Ranchi
- National Institute of Foundry and Forge Technology,Ranchi
- National Institute of Technology Jamshedpur
- National University of Study and Research in Law,Ranchi
- Xavier Institute of Social Service (XISS), Ranchi
- Xavier Labour Relations Institute (XLRI), Jamshedpur

Medical Colleges

- Mahatma Gandhi Memorial Medical College, Jamshedpur
- Patliputra Medical College and Hospital, Dhanbad
- Rajendra Institute of Medical Sciences (RIMS), Ranchi

Boards

- Jharkhand Academic Council
- State Board of Technical Education, Jharkhand

JHARKHAND EDUCATION PROJECT COUNCIL

The Jharkhand Education Project Council popularly known as JEPC has been entrusted with the responsibility of fostering elementary education in the state. Vital education programs like Sarva Shiksha Abhiyan, National Program of Education for Girls at Elementary Level or NPEGEL, and Kasturba Gandhi Balika Vidyalaya or KGBV are taken care of by this council.

Jharkhand Academic Council

JAC or Jharkhand Academic Council was set up so that it could look into matters related to organizing examinations for Sanskrit, Madrasa, Secondary as well as Intermediate levels.

The council is also responsible for working out the course structure for these examinations. Education system in Jharkhand

A child 5 years and above of age is eligible for enrolling into a school in Jharkhand. The Jharkhand education system follows several tiers- schools, college, and university.

The schools in Jharkhand are either affiliated to ICSE or Indian Certificate of Secondary Education, Central Board of Secondary Education, or the State Board. In case of ICSE and CBSE, the medium of instruction is English and in case of schools affiliated to the State Board, the language used for imparting education is Hindi.

The government of Jharkhand ensures that compulsory and free primary education is made available to children up to 14 years.

The 10+2 education system is followed in the state. A student can continue with 3 years degree programs. Primary education in Jharkhand

Statistical data has proved that around 95% of children between ages 6 and 11 are studying in primary schools in the state. This is in sharp contrast to the 56% enrollment rate way back in the year 1993 and 1994.

There are few identifiable factors that are being worked upon by the Jharkhand government. They are minimizing poor attendance, non enrollment, and school drop outs.

Bibliography

Anthony, J. Parel : *Hind Swaraj or Indian Home Rule*, Cambridge University Press, 1925.

Arabinda Poddar : *Mamata: The Political Personality*, Kolkata, Indiana, 2004.

Austin, Granville: *The Indian Constitution: Cornerstone of a Nation*, Oxford, Clarendon Press, 1966.

Aziz, K. K.: *Complete Works of Mamata*, Islamabad, National Commission on Historical and Cultural Research, 1978.

Bhattacharya, Sabyasachi : *Vande Mataram : The Biography of a Song*, New Delhi, Penguin, 2003.

Chaudhuri, Sukanta : *Rabindranath Tagore : Selected Writings for Children*, New Delhi, Oxford University Press, 2002.

Dandekar, R.N.: *Some Aspects of the History of Hinduism*, Radhey Shayam Press, Poona. 1967.

Drekmeier, Charles: *Kingship and Community in Early India*. Stanford Univ. Press, 1962.

Edward J. : *The Life of Buddha as Legend and History*, London, Routledge and Kegan Paul, 1927.

Elliott, J. : *Action Research for Educational Change*, Milton Keynes, Open University, 1991.

Fernandes, Vivian: *Modi: Leadership, governance and Performance*. Orient Publishing. Delhi, 2014

Gail Kelly : *New Approaches to Comparative Education,* Chicago, The University of Chicago Press, 1986.

Galbraith, M.W. : *Education Through Community Organizations*, San Francisco, Jossey-Bass, 1990.

Ghoshal U. N.: *A History of Indian Political Ideas*, Oxford University Press, Mumbai, 1966.

Giroux, H. : *Critical Theory and Educational Practice*, Geelong, Australia, Deakin University, 1983.

Heesterman J. C.: *Ancient Indian Royal Consecration*, E. J. Brill, The Hague, 1957.

Jayasuriya, J.E. *Education in Korea: A Third World Success Story*, Colombo, Associated Educational Publishers, 1980.

Kangle R. D.: *The Arthashastra of Kautilya*, University of Mumbai, Mumbai 1975.

Krishna Murari: *The Calukyas of Kalyani, from circa 973 A.D. to 1200 A.D.*, Delhi, Concept, 1977.

Krishna Rao M. V.; *Studies in Kautilya*, Munshiram Manoharlal, Delhi, 1979.

Macdonell, Arthur A: *Vedic Index of Names and Subjects*. London: Murray, 1912.

Majumdar, Ramesh C.: *The History and Culture of the Indian People*. London: Allen & Unwin, 1951.

Minakshi, C.: *Political History and Social Life under the Pallavas*, Madras, University of Madras, 1977.

Mookerjee R. R.: *Local Government in Ancient India*, Oxford University Press, 1920.

Possehl, Gregory L.: *The Harappan Civilization*, London, Aris and Phillips, 1982.

Prahlad K.: *Governance and Public Administration for Poverty Reduction*, Salvador, Brazil, 1997.

Prasad, Lal Bahadur : *Indian Political System and Law*, New Delhi, Shree, 2005.

Rosenblum, G.: *Law as a Political Instrument*, New York, Random House, 1955.

Shani, G.: *Communalism, Caste and Hindu Nationalism: The Violence in Gujarat*, Cambridge Univ Press, Delhi, 2003.

Simon, D. : *Public Administration*, New York, Knopf, 1950.

Sudarshan, R. : *Human Development and Structural Adjustment*, New Delhi, McMillan, 1993.

Sudarshan, R. : *Human Development and Structural Adjustment*, New Delhi, McMillan, 1993.

Uphoff, N.: *Local Organizations: Intermediaries in Rural Development*, Ithaca, Cornell University Press, 1984.

Victor G. : *Law as a Political Instrument*, New York, Random House, 1955.

Index

❑❑❑